Janna,

Thanks for all your
help and support with
this "Baby"!

Y<u>O</u>U are divine!

Rml Ch.
8/10/21

RECOGNITION FOR
SURVIVING THE DIVINE

"I once had a college professor who wished the astronauts were poets so they could more eloquently share their experience. But at least they took photographs. Describing spiritual experiences is more challenging because they are entirely subjective. The works of those who meet the challenge, such as St. Theresa of Avila or Patanjali, last for centuries or millennia. In this potential classic, Raphael Cushnir makes it clear that he's no saint or sage, but he writes with such clarity and candor that we become entrained to his experience of Kundalini awakening. He's also extremely honest and vulnerable. He divulges things that most of us would hesitate to tell our best friends. Is he crazy? Is he haunted by demons? Blessed by angels? All the above? Whatever he is, his experience is fascinating.

I had intended to skim this book to write this blurb but was immediately drawn in and read it cover to cover. Kundalini awakenings can be strange, frightening, destabilizing. They are also quite common and becoming more so as interest in experiential spirituality proliferates, even among some who are not pursuing it. Unfortunately, mental health professionals and the public know little or nothing about them. What might have been a profound spiritual transition with proper guidance and understanding instead often results in hospitalization and the administration of psychotropic medications. This book is an important contribution to our understanding of what kundalini awakenings are, how to manage them safely and use them as opportunities for tremendous growth."

—Rick Archer, host, *Buddha at the Gas Pump*

"I spend a lot of time counseling people who have had dramatic awakenings, and I can say that Raphael's account of his own incredibly targeted and subtle process will be of benefit to many. It's engagingly honest and a great read, and definitely helps advance our wisdom about Kundalini experience."

—Sally Kempton, author of *Awakening Shakti*
and *Meditation for the Love of It*

"I've never encountered a book quite like this one. Raphael's journey of awakening challenged me to rethink what awakening is all about. It's a courageous, fascinating tale of a difficult and complex journey into being. If you want to know more about what made Raphael the extraordinary teacher he is today, read this memoir!"

—Karen Brody, author of *Open Her*

"Like nothing I've ever read. Riveting, transparent, courageous, funny. Raphael's willingness to stay open to a very unsettling process of awakening—and then to be so honest about it—left me feeling expanded, thrilled, and somehow safe. It made me feel like there was more room in the world for me, and for my own 'off the map' experiences. It's an amazing story of someone's heart catching on fire, told in a way that scattered sparks all over my path."

—Tina Tau, author of *Ask for Horses*

"Raphael Cushnir is a great storyteller. His book reveals a dynamic and sometimes demonic interaction with Kundalini energy. Eventually he learns to navigate the relative and absolute elements of human experience through what he calls 'entwining the divine.' His story offers hope to others who have found themselves bewildered and besieged by the awakening process, and provides insight about this process for those who support experiencers."

—Bonnie Greenwell, PhD, non-dual teacher and author of
When Spirit Leaps: Navigating the Process of Spiritual Awakening
and *The Kundalini Guide*

"Raphael's story is one of trauma, perseverance, mystery, and grace. With love as his guide, aided by skilled discernment, his Kundalini process eventually matured from anguish to peace, enabling him to share his hard-earned understanding for the benefit of sincere, spiritually focused people. This book chronicles his extraordinary journey."

—Joan Shivarpita Harrigan, PhD, author of
Kundalini Vidya: The Science of Spiritual Transformation

"*Surviving the Divine* chronicles a strange and sacred love affair, a perilous adventure, a spiritual awakening, and a philosophical detective story. The shakti seized Raphael Cushnir, overwhelmed him and left him transformed. Beautifully written, this vivid, tender, hilarious, outrageous memoir is also an educational text, because it helps us all come to grounded terms with some of the wildest weirdness of our human and spiritual nature."

—Terry Patten, author of *A New Republic of the Heart,*
coauthor of *Integral Life Practice*

SURVIVING THE DIVINE
A Memoir of Rude Awakening

RAPHAEL CUSHNIR

Published in 2021 by As Above Books.
As Above Books
Portland, Oregon, USA

Cover illustration: *Leap of Faith*, copyright Mark Henson

Print ISBN: 978-1-09836-222-5
eBook ISBN: 978-1-09836-223-2

To all those whose spiritual journeys are as confounding as they are graceful. May you find the sacred space within to welcome it all.

We must accept our reality as vastly as we possibly can; everything, even the unprecedented, must be possible within it. This is in the end the only kind of courage that is required of us: the courage to face the strangest, most unusual, most inexplicable experiences that can meet us.

—Rainer Maria Rilke

INTRODUCTION

"The bigger the front, the bigger the back."

The first time I heard that proverb was in the 1980s from the poet and men's movement pioneer, Robert Bly. It has intrigued me ever since. Whenever people attempt to sell something, especially about themselves, there's always a dubious ring to it, even if we don't know the shadowy truth behind their "fronting." Taking the saying to heart, I wondered for many years if it was possible to share something personally meaningful with great passion, yet not to front at all.

Then it came to me. The only way to avoid the front/back dilemma was to create a circle. With a circle, there is no front or back. Nothing gets hidden or cleaned up. Everything is purposely included in order to create the most complete, authentic expression.

The story I'm about to tell is full circle. Whenever I felt a temptation to leave something out, that urge almost always redirected me to leave it in. I need to share this at the outset because the story is largely unbelievable. No doubt it has the potential to surprise, scare, confront, and confuse.

"There are more things in heaven and earth, Horatio, than are dreamt of in your philosophy."

The first time I read this Shakespearean epigram I knew instantly that it was true for me. I just had no idea *how* true. This book is about what happened when a spontaneous, cataclysmic, cosmic force swept through me. The experience was nothing at all like familiar stories of divine revelation.

It was almost impossible to endure. It was also exquisite, mesmerizing, a deliverance of grace that I never wanted to end.

It hasn't. Going on twenty-five years.

This story mostly covers how it all began, and what I had to do to survive and stay sane. Its main focus is 1995–2000, the years before I wholly transformed my life to become a writer and teacher of emotional connection, present moment awareness, and spiritual liberation.

The years between then and now, when I was on the tail end of the cataclysm, are perhaps the focus of a follow-up volume. Here, I aim for the fullest possible rendering of the initial holy mess, a roaring fire of torment that consumed nearly everything in its path and paved the way for what came next.

There are many descriptions across different cultures for the first spiritual spark that began my journey. There's *ruach* from Judaism, *loa* from Voudoun, *tummo* from Tibetan Buddhism, Holy Spirit from Christianity, and, with the most extensive body of accounts and scholarly research, *Kundalini* from the Hindu tradition. There are numerous symbols that depict it as well, such as a serpent, a cross, and serpents wrapped around a cross.

But all of those are just names and images. They don't come anywhere close to capturing the experience itself, whether for me or for any other individual to whom it actually happens. Plus, no two people experience it the same way. For the sake of convenience, going forward, I'll use the term "Kundalini awakening" to refer to it. Sometimes I'll just call its manifestation "the energy." But whatever I call it, I'll do so with reluctance at the inevitable diminishment of mystery that results.

One thing I want to make clear at the outset is that I'm not talking about God, if that term is meant to suggest the Absolute, something beyond form, emptiness, and comprehension. Instead, the spiritual spark I'm describing seems to blast through the barriers of ordinary consciousness that keep us distant and disconnected *from* God—or Source, Pure Awareness, True Nature, whatever designation we prefer.

This breach may take the form of an invitation, an initiation, or even a brutish intrusion. Suddenly we're closer to God, or rather an emanation of God, and somehow it's not just happening to us but it's also *relating* to us. It's both the message and the messenger all at once. In the throes of this relationship we're also stripped of almost everything familiar. Our lives still unfold as before, but in a whole new universe as baffling as it is beatific.

Engaging with this new universe changed my most basic perceptions of the previous universe I had inhabited for thirty-five years. And it changed me too, fundamentally, in ways that took till now to fully comprehend, accept, and share.

In the year 2000, I published my first book, *Unconditional Bliss*, drawn from my Kundalini awakening. It focused on my lessons learned from the cat-aclysm, and how they could help the reader find greater peace and well-being. Notably absent was any detailed description of the awakening itself. Why? In part, I feared that it would distract from the principles and practices I dearly wanted to impart. I also feared ridicule, shaming, and being written off as just one more New Age nutcase. Furthermore, I dutifully heeded all the warnings in mystical traditions not to dwell on the distracting "fireworks" that may occur along the path.

I still stand by that book, but also recognize that in some ways it was premature. Before I had even tested out the book's principles and practices with individuals and groups, I was blithely promising their benefits. It all worked out, and soon enough I was traveling the world and sharing the work with thousands of people. Still, even if well meaning, even if entirely appropriate, this omission of what actually happened to me was a kind of fronting.

If that first book was premature, this one might be long overdue. Many of my fears about including everything were unfounded, mostly generated to protect my ego and control the way other people saw me. A desire to be liked, understood, seen as wise and trustworthy clouded my perception.

Now, as I like to say, "I'll be gone soon." With good fortune that will be within decades not years, yet as I conclude my sixtieth year I've pretty much stopped editing myself based on the fear of what other people may think.

Plus, this book isn't written for the vast majority of people. Most would have no interest in it, denounce it, or just come away befuddled. As much as I sometimes wish my story was one of those classic triumphs over adversity, a tale that through its particulars becomes universal, I've resigned myself to the fact that it's probably just not. It also seems unlikely and inadvisable to try to shoehorn it into such a form. Instead, it's written specifically for people who are tired of fronting when it comes to the spiritual life, who yearn for a mysticism that's as complex, grounded, and nuanced as they are.

Hopefully, that's you.

If it is you, it's likely that you've long been intrigued by mystical encounters. Perhaps you've had some of your own, Kundalini related or otherwise. They may have been spontaneous or sought after via psychedelics. However your encounters came about, they may have occurred as a "still, small voice" or as a full-on explosion. You may have shared them or stayed mum. They may have gradually integrated with the rest of your life or remained anomalous. Either way, their indelible arising no doubt piqued your curiosity about what more lies behind the veils of ordinary perception.

When the veils part, the resulting encounters may span the spectrum from ecstatic to horrific, clear to confounding. Often, as it was for me, they're a blend. Traditions and teachers offer an abundance of advice about whether such encounters are real or illusory, safe or dangerous, meaningful or insignificant. Yet such encounters are largely subjective, which means no external adviser can make a precise, definitive evaluation.

In the thick of it, therefore, you may find yourself at one with the universe while at the same time utterly alone. When that happens, evaluation and advice can't usually reach you anyway. The only thing that can, for sure, is communion. By communion I mean the reassurance that what you're experiencing matters, that others care enough to suspend their own judgments and really listen to you, that they're willing to stay with you through all your inevitable stumbles.

Why do I stress this? How does it apply to this book? The best way to answer these questions is to describe what occurred when I shared a draft of the book with a small group of people I considered representative readers. While some found great value in the story, others urged me not to publish it. Those in the don't-publish camp found many details of my encounters off-putting. They deemed some of my responses to the phenomena misguided, unhelpful, and signs of an *un*awakened mind.

"We love you," began their imploring. "The trust and acceptance you facilitate in your gatherings is what drew us to you, and what we value most about you. But if we had read this book before meeting you, we never would have signed up. Why tell this story if it's going to turn away people who could otherwise gain so much from what you have to offer?"

I'll admit it—this perspective gave me pause. I treasure the opportunity I've been granted to help people heal and realize their spiritual wholeness. I don't take jeopardizing that opportunity at all lightly. Yet it's through my transformation story that this sacred opportunity arose in the first place. The two are inextricably connected, and I've come to believe that revealing what happened to me in an unvarnished way may be not just an opportunity, but also a responsibility.

In deference to the don't-publish camp, I freely admit that some of my responses to the phenomena might indeed have been misguided, unhelpful, and signs of an unawakened mind. That's because it's impossible to always be awakened while awaken*ing*. As I see it, my responsibility in chronicling these events is not to soften, tidy, or predigest the bedlam. Especially, I need to render the person I was during that bedlam in all his neurotic splendor.

Many awakeners and would-be awakeners, I believe, are a lot like I was. In the midst of the mystery, with no clear path forward and no one to reliably lead the way, they may cling to their habits, defenses, and projections. The more bewildering things get, the more they may regress. They may temporarily become delirious and inflated, mistaking derangement for spiritual progress. All this ego flailing may be unavoidable. It may even be an intrinsic part of the awakening process.

I'm guided to share my own version of that process, flailing and all, in communion with those who may find themselves in similar terrain. And if I lose a few potential workshop participants in the telling, so be it.

That said, I do want to take a moment to address the continuum between privacy and transparency. Whenever possible, I tend more toward transparency. That's a requirement of the full-circle approach, and it also takes into account the grave harm many spiritual leaders create when acting out their unacknowledged shadows.

At the same time, I'm aware that there are many things we don't want or need to know about those who guide us. Some of those things might even compromise the healing relationship, and thereby jeopardize our ability to grow.

If you happen to be a client or workshop participant of mine, past or present, you know that I value your sense of safety with me above all. In keeping with that value, it's important to let you know that this particular book calls for a heightened degree of transparency. Though my hope is that everyone will come away from it feeling even safer with me, it's possible that for some it will be too much. So if you don't want to risk the healing relationship we have, and you're not 100 percent sure about reading on, I'd suggest erring on the side of caution.

Another challenge I faced in presenting my story, even before the very first draft, was how in the world to approach it. I couldn't write the book in a self-help style, because that would flatten the events beyond recognition. I also couldn't just present the events in straightforward prose, because that would seem to make sense out of what remains for me, to this day, something entirely nonrational.

What finally broke the stylistic logjam was the idea that I could match the messiness of the experience with an equally messy rendition. I could address the reader, myself, and also the energy directly. I could include prose and poetry both, letting them portray the same events from vastly different angles. I could present unedited journal entries from that time, and also surround them with commentaries from today. I could relate what happened from the viewpoint of not just one coherent self but from the many selves that actually vie within me. And perhaps most important, I could share the doubts and struggles about presenting this material that came up for me while writing it, therefore creating a full circle that includes not just my subject but also my process.

It's that freedom to be all over the place that got me going, and kept me at it, through a three-month sabbatical and then two years more.

One last thing before diving in. This love affair with Spirit would never have caught fire outside the crucible of my love for an actual flesh-and-blood woman. That love, for the one whom here I'll call Hannah, was blessed and doomed in equal measure. These pages will reveal almost as much about our union as they will about the energy and me. While the union was brief, the heartbreak was unrelenting. Which is the greatest gift anyone ever could have given me. No heartbreak, no heart opening.

So Hannah, thank you, from the bottom of my open heart.

1

I need to write about You. I don't know how. I don't even know how to refer to You. Hallowed seems too dry, sacred too careful. There are no words that capture You, or even just evoke You without getting it all wrong. Internal or external? Masculine or feminine? Every classification is blasphemy. Every name, at best, misleads.

Maybe I should just stop, shut up about us. That's what they say. It's just fireworks, not the real fire. Don't get lost in it. Don't distract yourself from what really matters. Don't create a sense of longing in others, of lack, by crowing about your story.

But it is my story. And it did happen. We happened. And we keep happening. It feels just as wrong to stay quiet, to hide our holy love affair. How could I possibly do that? It would be like trying not to breathe.

Out of all the one-plus-ones, we're another. No better, or worse, just different. But I can't shake this calling to bear witness. If I died with us hidden inside me, it would be a bad death. A stillbirth.

So I've canceled my life for a while. I've cleared the calendar. There's nothing but us now.

I apologize in advance for the colossal failure this will inevitably become. But I also promise to let it bring me to my knees. To scrape at the truth of us till I'm raw and spent, to clean up nothing in my description, to slay my pride when it tries to make us look good; or, more to the point, when it tries to make me look good.

◆

What is he talking about?

It sounds so pompous.

Our entire respectability is at stake—

The whole inner committee—

After decades of investing in it.

We are wise.

We've made him wise.

This mania—or whatever it is—just isn't acceptable.

But he seems hell-bent.

Will anything dissuade him?

Think. Think!

◆

When I was seven years old, I lay in my bed on Sunday mornings and stared up at the cottage cheese ceiling. The puffy specks would turn into a rainbow of color and begin moving. It was as if they were little people, gliding along town streets to a cathedral at the center. I remember some kind of choral music in the background, too. The whole tableau was pulsing, radiant, solemn in a way that was both haunting and soothing at once.

I was frozen in awe. Honored to see.

But what exactly was I seeing? A wish? A nostalgic hallucination? Some kind of bleed-through from another dimension? Was it significant or random? Was there any way to tell? I felt safe, and sane, but was I really?

◆

If I hadn't met Hannah, I never would have met You either. She was my raft to the underworld, my trickster demon, my dark inside the light. Her pain was worse than my pain. It humbled and entranced me. I was frozen in awe. Stung.

She insisted that for our wedding, my first and her second, that the gown would not be white. We both loved a store called CP Shades that specialized in lush natural fabrics. Romantic treasure hunter that I am, I sought out the owners and wrote them a paean to their forest-green velvet. I implored them to sell us a bolt. It worked. Then I found a friend of a friend to sew a custom dress. Hannah adored the dress and everything that went into creating it. She felt humbled and beguiled by my devotion. Loved in a whole new way.

There's a photo of Hannah wearing that gown on our wedding day, just an hour before the ceremony. For some reason, the photographer blew that particular picture up to a full 18 by 24 inches.

Actually, I know why she blew it up. Hannah looks achingly beautiful in it. Her black curls waterfall perfectly onto the velvet. Though there is not a drop of Spanish blood within her, she gazes directly into the lens like a smoldering flamenco queen.

For the year and a half after the wedding I would show off the picture to anyone who visited. I could never believe I landed someone so intensely ravishing. This woman was serious. She didn't take anything lightly, especially marrying me.

But for all I saw or read into the photo, I missed the most crucial feature. Only after everything happened, and a few months before I met You, did I truly get what she was trying to tell me.

I am here, my love, to destroy you.

◆

In the beginning was the word. With the word came creation, but also separation. A name is not the thing, a map is not the territory. To talk about anything, to write about it, is to be on the outside.

Words create stories, and stories create worlds. We immerse ourselves in those worlds as if they're real, as if they make us real. We learn to tell our own stories in order to take up space, to find our rightful place. We disappear into the stories of others—legends, novels, memoirs, films—in order to see ourselves anew, to feel ourselves anew. Story worlds give birth, and rebirth, because looking and telling from the outside is the best way we have of inhabiting the inside.

Or is it? Every story is in part an origin story. "This is where I come from. This is who I am," the story proclaims, blind to the inevitable separation that bedevils it. Once you tell a story, it's no longer alive in the same way. The more you believe your *own* story, the more rigid you become.

Seekers ask: Who would I be without my stories?

Meditators watch: What happens when I stop investing in my stories? What they find, amazingly, alarmingly, is that the stories keep telling themselves. The words and thoughts and beliefs and interpretations that make up our stories turn out to be on autopilot, fabricated in the unconscious and cast upon our conscious minds whether we like it or not.

Creating, separating, creating, separating—story worlds run on an endless loop baked right into our nature. Deny them at your peril. They're like that Chinese finger trap: the more you try to pull your finger out, the tighter it gets locked in.

Stop trying, stop pulling, and what happens? Maybe nothing, if you just sit there and wait. But in that pause, that oh-so-pregnant pause, a new impulse may arise. Instead of pulling away, trying to get out, would it be possible to push in? Doing so, it turns out, is the only way to wrest your finger free.

The chance to transcend the separation that stories create, to return to life, to the inside, comes from diving fully back into them. From looking at their components with passionate curiosity. Watching, waiting, penetrating further and further into the very marrow out of which stories are formed.

A chair, viewed through an electron microscope, turns out to be an endless dance of atomic particles.

A story, viewed with similar magnification, falls apart into its essence. That essence can never be named or instantly, the whole story world reconfigures to obscure it once again. Even talking about it scatters the essence back into separation.

To experience our own essence, to live in accord with it, we must, strange as it seems, relax.

Push in and let go. Look at everything, but for nothing in particular. Let our looking become so passionate that it overtakes us, that we can't even distinguish the seer from what we see.

Sometimes we stumble upon such looking by accident, like a seven-year-old boy in his Sunday morning reverie.

Sometimes we refuse to see, clinging to our story world with such ferocity that absolutely nothing can pry us free. Nothing, that is, except complete annihilation at the hand of one we cherish.

I am here, my love, to destroy you.

◆

As I tell you this story, please don't believe me. It's all true (although I changed the names of the key players to protect their privacy), but that doesn't matter. What matters is that you look into it, relax into it, and maybe, just maybe, fall apart into it.

◆

This is getting worse!

Veering toward bossy and pretentious.

Why can't he just tell the story and stop framing it?

People want to have their own reading experience, not be led through it on a leash.

It's just like him, not leaving well enough alone.

What leverage do we have to rein him in?

Think! Think!

◆

When the student is ready, the teacher will appear. Or so the saying goes. But sometimes the teacher appears before the student is ready. Or sometimes the teacher is so incredibly bizarre that it's impossible to take the lessons seriously.

Luisa grew up in Beverly Hills, California, rebelled against her privilege, and became an acupuncturist in the nearby bohemian enclave of Topanga Canyon. We were lovers for a short time when I was in my twenties, and I would visit her in a tiny cottage she rented amid the dusty sun and eucalyptus.

I was attracted to her fearless brilliance, and equally put off by where it led. She stored raw beef kidneys in her fridge for times when she was "yang deficient." She would tackle me in the meadow by her house, no matter the mood, because suddenly she just felt like it.

I would often get flooded, trapped by the vehemence of Luisa's impulses. I didn't know how to just say, "This is too much! You're freaking me out!" I judged my revulsion as small-minded, rigid, and so most of the time pretended to be cool with everything.

One time I accompanied her to an appointment for some "energy work." I didn't yet know what that was. I sat quietly nearby as she lay on a massage table while a friend ran her hands up and down Luisa's body. After a few minutes, Luisa began to writhe and tremble, to stutter and moan as if she was speaking in tongues.

I thought something might be wrong, especially as it went on for what seemed like forever, but neither Luisa nor her friend expressed any concern.

"Your Shakti is so strong today," the friend said.

"I know," Luisa whispered, giggling with delight.

To be honest, I thought she was faking. Or that she was captive to a New Age delusion. Or showing off. Or purposely trying to freak me out.

My own mystical yearning was chastened by groundedness, and a formidable bullshit detector. Somewhere along the way I read a quote from the Buddha that warned us not to believe anything we haven't experienced directly. Seemed about right.

But there was Luisa, still twitching and gurgling on the table. The sight of her nagged at me. What if it *was* real? What would it mean? How would my worldview need to shift to make space for something so outlandish?

More to the point, what would make a body do that? What was the relationship between her friend's hands, which weren't even touching Luisa, and all that shaking?

I had no answers to any of those questions. And, back then, it all really was too much. So I broke up with Luisa soon after and tried to shelve the whole conundrum.

My shelving was successful for the most part, until my therapist at the time, Rebecca (more about her later), suggested that I visit a nearby healer. Rebecca told me nothing about what to expect, which in retrospect was an odd choice.

Following the street directions to the appointment, I found myself in a large trailer park. That alone threw me for a loop, but nonetheless I climbed the steps of the designated mobile home and knocked on its aluminum door. The healer ushered me in with a slow wave. She a was a kindly grandmother type who spoke in a charming Scottish brogue. I'll call her Agnes, since I don't remember her actual name.

Agnes pointed out a bulletin board festooned with Polaroids of her satisfied customers. They seemed to be a wide array of ordinary folks, so I relaxed a little and lay down on my back as instructed.

Then Agnes explained that her healing treatment would locate and extract any unwanted vibrations from my system. What she didn't explain was the form in which the extraction would take place.

As Agnes circled the bed like a detective, suddenly she began to belch. And wretch. And fart. Apparently, the bad stuff that she sniffed out needed to move through me to her, and it was necessary for her to then expel it once and for all in this crude, earthy way.

Part of me remained a dutiful client, hoping the session would help with some of my physical ailments. Another part was totally aghast, miffed at both Agnes and Rebecca for not giving me even a minimal heads-up. Was I supposed to consider this normal? To just brush it off? Still another part of me thought it was hysterical, and wanted to remember every possible detail in order to tell the story later.

The belch-wretch-fart routine lasted for about a half hour. It included brief periods of silence along the way, each followed by an even more thunderous purging than the last. Then, unceremoniously, it was over. I wrote a check and handed it to Agnes, who gave me a reassuring hug and sent me on my way.

I never returned for another session, or experienced any conscious benefit from the treatment. At the time I had no way of knowing that my subsequent journey into the esoteric, by comparison, would render Agnes's antics as harmlessly quaint.

◆

Hannah, like Luisa, was an acupuncturist. I met her a few years later. In addition to her doctorate in oriental medicine, she was also a PhD candidate in clinical psychology and an actress who almost made it big. Her blend of intellectual rigor, artistic talent, and deeply soothing warmth were irresistible to me. Those same subtle energies that in Luisa seemed only kooky, Hannah actually made a case for in a completely grounded way.

This time I was open, ready to learn. And to be loved in a whole new way.

The old love, if it can be called that, was the soup in which I first swam. Neither my mother nor father knew how to bond. In turn, as I later came to understand, I wasn't able to bond with them. They provided well and offered me ample opportunity to grow and prosper, but inside their fulfillment of duty it was barren, bitter, and corroded with rage. Dad took his rage out on Mom, and Mom took hers out on her kids.

How much of this is necessary to share? I'm not sure, but maybe just one of their usual go-rounds will suffice.

Mom would inadvertently diminish Dad. Dad would explode at Mom, then stop talking to her for weeks on end. His only communication was about when he'd be home for dinner—which had better be on the table. No discussion of the inciting offense was allowed.

During this time Mom would be helpless and miserable, which she couldn't keep from spewing onto us siblings. Sometimes it would take the form of competition for scarce resources:

"How could you be so ungrateful?! Do you know what I could have bought myself with the cost of your jacket?!"

Often it was blatant shaming, like when the ball rolled into her flower bed:

"How dare you! Goddamn you! Everything you touch turns to dirt!"

All four of us kids knew how over the top this was, and whenever possible we made light of it. But that was just as lethal, in its own way, because it led us to believe that we weren't actually ripped up by her tirades.

When Dad decided Mom's punishment was over, he brought home flowers and gave them to her with a spooky "It's all good" grin. As if none of it had ever happened. If Mom risked a question about how they could avoid it next time, he'd go dark and threaten to start all over again.

This was the '60s. Underneath her fury, Mom was terrified, dependent, and unwilling to risk divorce. Which left her, and the rest of us, without any options.

Between rounds of this cycle, neither Mom nor Dad ever offered a hug, or said "I love you" to any of us. Ever. If they had, it would have felt awkward and forced. We wouldn't have trusted it.

Each of us developed our own defense against this battleground, as well as our own dysfunction. My primary poison was to spurn any type of healthy relationship and instead to seek love wherever it couldn't be found. This replication of my upbringing was unconscious, for sure, but executed to perfection.

I specialized in girls who were like wounded birds. I would tend to them with great care, restore them to flight, fully expecting every time that they would glide back into my arms rather than revel in their newfound strength and freedom. Even if they wanted to fall for me, they couldn't. My love was destined to be unrequited. It was the state I knew best of all.

Until Hannah. Though wounded, she wouldn't let me fix her. She actually fixed me, over and over. And I actually let her. This was brand new territory, irresistible and intoxicating.

Not that I went down without a fight. I kept tweaking the terms of our commitment, angling for possible gray areas and free passes. And I wasn't shy about my resistance to settling in. One night we were scheduled for a date, but I was irritable and suggested that it would be better for me to cocoon. Hannah was understanding, kind, and let me know that I was welcome to come over no matter my state, to interact in whatever way felt best, even if that meant adjacent cocoons.

This simple idea—that I might be acceptable as I was, surliness and all, without evoking attack and blame—was a revelation to me. I took Hannah up on her offer and drove over. I remember melting at her soft smile on the apartment stairway. No surliness anywhere within me. Suddenly I just wanted to be close.

2

O, Holy One, I can feel You straining against all this biography. *None of it matters. Get wild, already. Show them who we are.*

But, I humbly protest, I'm half the union. There's no us without me. If I leave all this out, what's left is merely a roaring, scorching void. No on-ramp to make any of it approachable. No story to fall apart into.

There's another reason I have to include so much, excruciating though it may be for both of us. In all the conflicting literature about *Shakti* and Kundalini, one consistent concept rings true. When the divine light ignites, and begins to burn its way through every karmic knot, any amount of illumination that can't penetrate those knots spills from the sacred channels into the individual's subconscious. Once there, it can create *kriyas*, the term for involuntary movements and sounds, and can also accentuate whatever is still rough and unintegrated from one's personal and archetypal identity. The sparks land randomly, projecting flashes of a mystifying, sometimes insane-seeming inner movie. Martin (we'll get to him later) called this my Spiritual Disneyland.

Whatever we call it, it's how You messed with me.

If I dare say.

It's tempting, therefore, to leave it all out as distracting and irrelevant detail.

But it's almost always left out. Sometimes due to religious, moral, or cultural proscription, other times due to embarrassment or fear of reprisal.

The sex, especially, gets edited or fuzzed beyond recognition. When I read Gopi Krishna's famous account of his own ordeal, *Living with Kundalini*, I wanted to scream, "Stop being so vague! So clinical! Just say what happened, and how it impacted you personally. Talk about sexuality as fully and clearly as you do every other aspect of your experience."

So I have to share the gore, every manner of it. Otherwise I join the lie of omission, of obfuscation.

It's not that our love is special, higher or better, or that the details of our particular explosion are significant in themselves. It's that You only love one at a time. You see Your own face anew in each of us. We, likewise, touch the hem of Your garment with hands uniquely calloused and scarred. The blessing of Your Grace is eternal, yes, but also, and always, original.

O, Holy One, may I bear full, chaotic, mortifying witness to our love. May my offering attune others to the uniqueness of their own divine encounter. When You come to each of them, no matter how confounding the guise, no matter how painful the fallout, may they recognize Your Awesome Presence and bow. Not run.

◆

In the Book of Genesis, Jacob spends a whole night wrestling with an angel. Afterward he is blessed and calls the site of the struggle *Peniel*, or "Face of God."

Seems about right.

◆

When my father got really mad at me, he'd yell, "Go to your room with no clothes on!" Such naked banishment was common. In later years my father told me that he had no idea where it came from or what it was supposed to accomplish.

Another jolt of shame, most likely, but it also turned out to have the opposite effect. At these times I was alone with my body. The rainbow village on the ceiling would respectfully fade to white. In this private purgatory I would stretch, pose, roll around, gaze at myself in the mirror, luxuriate. My hands would wander, find new thrills. Pleasure was punishment. Punishment was pleasure.

Did this kink me in some way? I don't know. I never identified like that. But I need to touch on the subject here because of how, thirty years later, in the searing light of Grace, sexuality and ecstasy came to take on some surprisingly dark dimensions.

Long before that, however, things had already become confusing. During my teenage years, the unrequited wounded-bird theme was already in full effect. My fragile heart was a wreck, and desire was inseparable from rejection. But on my own, exploring sexual frontiers was also incredibly soothing. Plus, in a way that felt at least as spiritual as it did sexual, I longed to merge with everything, alive and inanimate, real and imaginary. I didn't know anything then about the primal power of Eros, but I was clearly in its grip.

In my twenties, finally finding partners who matched my enthusiasm, I flirted with many flavors. Was I fully straight? Bi? Dominant? Submissive? All the while, it was rare for sex and love to go together. That's what I truly wanted, but most of my liaisons would flame out quickly. Someone would accidentally become vulnerable, get hurt, and that would be the end of that.

By the time I reached Hannah, at age thirty-one, I spurned "vanilla" and dared anyone interested in me to match my carnal edge. She didn't laugh in my face, but given her own history, she could have.

Sexually abused by her mother, Hannah briefly became a teen prostitute. It came about by accident when a boy from a neighboring town offered her money for service. Something in her own wrecked heart found this fitting, so she agreed, and word got around. In her hometown, Hannah was a model student and a budding starlet. One town over she was the Whore of Babylon.

In the realm of sex, and way beyond, this gave Hannah cred with me. Not the prostitution itself, but how much trauma must have been necessary just for her to consider the possibility. And then, what had she done since? Years of therapy in the pursuit of self-understanding and acceptance, extensive training to transform her pain into artistic expression, and then the remarkable decision to channel all her brilliance toward the physical and emotional healing of others.

This grit and resilience floored me. I wanted to own that in myself. I wanted us to stand for it together. I envisioned us as the brave ones, able to triumph over our tragedies and embrace every shade of life, no matter how dark. But my need to see us in this way also blinded me to what didn't fit that narrative.

Hannah's healing journey definitely wasn't a straight line. She had attempted suicide three times. Her last attempt had occurred just nine months before we met.

Perhaps it's more accurate to say that I did see all that, but discounted it. I assumed, tragically, that it was no match for our love.

Looking back, my mammoth missteps are all too clear. Had I not been so overblown, it would have been possible to find, heed, and speak to my underlying fear.

I believe in you, honey, but your tenuous hold on life concerns me. It's not something I've ever dealt with. I don't know how to include it, to feel safe with it as the two of us grow closer.

Had I not been so obsessed with protecting Hannah's feelings, it would have been possible for me to offer practical suggestions.

I believe in us, honey, which is why I think we should see a counselor about this issue. Having someone to help us explore it, to offer reflection and guidance, would be so helpful to me. At least till we're on more solid ground.

But these are course corrections I couldn't yet manage. Which rendered Hannah, for her part, my greatest wounded bird of all. Unhealed but glorious, she took refuge in my arms and stayed. Until she didn't.

◆

By the time I said goodbye to Hannah, You and I had already been together for two years. I literally pulsed with You. My breath was a bellows, stoking a fire in my heart fueled by joy. Endless joy. Beginningless joy. Infatuation with everything. But also with nothing, and especially no one, in particular.

Reverence, unintentional and effortless, was the path beneath me and the cloak around me. As long as I stayed out of Your way, and let You lead, there was never a problem. Nothing was wrong. Anywhere. Every speck of creation was simply, profoundly perfect.

But even then, saying goodbye to Hannah was nearly impossible. Even after the affair, all the lies, the fourth attempt, the psych ward, I clung to her like a fossilized barnacle.

Why? Finally, I knew. Hannah represented all those who had ever suffered. To leave her would mean turning my back on all the innocents who had been victimized, brutalized by life. It wasn't her fault she had been abused. It was doubly cruel that persistent childhood trauma—one of the worst hands that a person could be dealt—inevitably led to an adulthood on repeat. The same shit over and over. From every angle. Try being the abuser this time. How's that? Not much better, huh?

No! This couldn't be. I wouldn't let it.

Turned out there was still a problem after all.

The reason I was finally able to let Hannah go, to both choose and follow through with it after so many previous stumbles, was that I had seen through the insanity of my projection. Hannah was just a person. She didn't represent anything. The problem had always been me. The whole wounded-bird thing, my decades of fervent activism on behalf of the oppressed, it had all been an outsourcing of my own vulnerability. My own trauma. My own victimization.

I couldn't face and embrace all that within, so I unconsciously barnacled to it outside of me as a way to stay close.

Bolstered by this recognition, uplifted by Your radiance, I began the practice of taking myself back. Each time I was drawn toward Hannah's pain, toward the siren song of saving her, I would locate the corollary pain in my own gut. I would cradle that pain with gentle attention. I would stay attuned to it, like I'd never been able to before, till it would begin to soften and disperse.

This practice would usually take about two or three minutes. Afterward I would feel soulful, relieved, reprieved. I repeated the practice about twenty times a day, for a few weeks, until the last cord was fully cut.

This practice, years later, also provided the template for what I came to call "Living the Questions." *What is happening right now? Can I be with it?* Asking those two questions over and over, with a focus on the body, is the best way I know to recognize and release resistance, to stay present when it's hardest, and to ride out even the most difficult emotions.

At the time, I didn't Live the Questions on purpose. I stumbled into them, or perhaps You nudged me toward them. I had no idea that they would become the heart of my first book, or that I would travel the world teaching them. All I know now is that when I was finally ready to heal, they healed me.

◆

Let me settle all this down, time-wise, to avoid any unnecessary confusion. I met Hannah in 1991, when I was thirty-one. We married in 1993, then separated in 1995. Nine months after that is when the energy woke up in me, and my inner relationship with it began. A year and a half later Hannah and I officially divorced, while my relationship with the energy has continued to this day.

It's easy to see, from the events of the early '90s that I'm about to fill in, how my commitment to emotional surrender played a key role in unleashing the energy. But what prepared me for that surrender, ironically, was a whole lot of *not* letting go. I guess you could say I was a serial not-let-goer.

The first time set the stage for all the others that followed. It showed me, to my grateful surprise, that I was actually capable of real change.

When Hannah and I began dating, we agreed upon a kind of loose monogamy. We could be physical with other people above the belt and didn't have to report it, but anything below the belt required full disclosure. At first this freedom helped me stay connected to Hannah, even though I didn't take advantage of it. But then, in an act of obvious self-sabotage, I crossed the line.

It was tempting to keep this transgression to myself, but I respected Hannah too much to deceive her, and I knew that in such a circumstance I would also lose respect for myself. Not to mention the guilt. So, sick to my stomach, I sucked it up and told her what had happened.

Predictably, she was upset. Not because I did something wrong—I hadn't—but because it spoke to something in me that couldn't be satisfied with just us. She suggested that we break it off right then, because there was only more hurt ahead in any type of joint future. Hearing her, sensing the enormity of what I had to lose, I shocked myself with vehement disagreement. I told her I would change. She said people don't really change. I promised her, in this case, that wouldn't be true. I agreed that she shouldn't take it on faith, but instead should watch me over the next six months and judge for herself.

She remained hesitant. I wore her down. Eventually, she relented.

Now I really had to come through. And I did, with one misstep, a kind of final, before-the-betrothal goodbye to all that. I was pretty sure she sensed it. I, too, sensed that she'd had some missteps of her own, out of revenge, or to balance the playing field—I didn't want to probe or know for sure.

Then we went to see the Disney movie *Aladdin*. Scarred and jaded though we were, it touched a pure, innocent place in both of us. Afterward, we walked through the parking structure singing "Whole New World" at the top of our lungs. Laughing, melting, not ready to face any potential rupture that might come from talking things through, we circled the car and kept singing.

Then I had an idea. Tentatively, I floated it. What if the last few months didn't count? What if we each got a pass? What if we let this indelible wave of sweetness wash us clean and surge us forward?

It turned out she wanted this as much as I did. So that's what happened. The wave carried us through engagement, moving out of Los Angeles, starting a new life in the Bay Area, and getting married on Thanksgiving Day at a rustic inn above the ocean surrounded by a small group of family and friends who all saw for themselves that we were made for each other.

Not letting go. Round One concluded. On the other side of that wave, I was all in. Not only was I free of doubt and roving attention, but I was so relieved at the transformation that I celebrated it with Hannah, giddily, every day.

Which is why I was so taken aback when she sat me down and intoned solemnly, "I know that one day you're going to betray me. If it happens when you're off directing a movie, with some ingenue, and if you're sure it's not a threat to our relationship, I don't need to know about it."

There are so many possible ways to respond to such a statement. Mine was the dumbest. Instead of asking where this all came from, or wondering if she was really talking about herself, or just saying, "No, I'm not going to do that," I muttered something like, "Cool. Okay. Same for you."

I guess I thought the *Aladdin* wave was still lifting us up. But it wasn't.

A few months later, Hannah called me from her office and said she had to come home right away. Her voice sounded doomed. I asked if it was really bad. She said yes.

Here's how I wrote about what happened next in the December 2002 issue of *O, The Oprah Magazine:*

In the 20 minutes it took for Hannah to arrive, I sat on the porch trying to imagine what had happened. Was it about illness? Work? Money? Hannah pulled into the driveway, and I followed her inside. She looked me in the eye for a split second, then looked away. "I'm having an affair," she said. "I don't think I can stop."

There it was. The single thing I had never considered. For the next three months, as we separated, I was utterly lost. Every moment felt like a punch in the gut.

That account was true. It was also selective, reductive, and tilted toward the needs of a "teaching" story about finding peace amid great pain. What's more compelling to me at this point, absent the desire to teach, is what I left out. In reality, it wasn't the affair that laid me low. Hannah explained that it was meant to be a one-night stand, sanctioned by our now stupid-seeming mutual agreement about such events. The rest—falling in love with Alex, struggling to end it—was as mortifying to her as it was accidental.

A soon as I learned all this, I suggested we hurry to a counselor and try to repair our cracked container. I was such a robust believer in the tools of therapy that I thought simply applying them would swiftly and efficiently save us. I was deeply wounded, yes, but also ready and able to do my part. I trusted Hannah to do hers as well.

If she could have, she would have. I believed that then, and I believe it now.

What actually did lay me low happened a month later. By this point she had left me and our two cats and moved in with Alex across town. She'd stopped by to pick up some of her stuff. We sat together on the couch. She could barely look at me. She was distraught, shaking. I said to her, "When you married me, you became my family. You don't get kicked out of my family unless that's what you want. So tell me, in your heart of hearts, what you really want."

Hannah heard the urgency of my plea and honored it. She took a long time to respond, to find the most accurate words.

"All I want," she told me, "is to be with you. I know that seems insane right now, since I'm living with another man. I know it seems like I have all the power in this situation, but the truth is I feel powerless. I feel like all of this is happening *to* me and I can't do anything to stop it. I see the possibility of you and me getting back together as a dim light at the end of a long tunnel. I can't say for sure that I'll ever get there, and I would never ask you to wait for me, but that's what's in my heart of hearts."

The combination of my unwavering love for her, the desperation in her eyes, and my still unchallenged need to save her, to save everyone, kept me from fleeing. If she had to go all the way down, to hit bottom before resurfacing, I'd valiantly hold her spot—our spot—above ground for as long as it took.

Not letting go. Round Two in full effect.

Not letting go, however, didn't lead to any kind of equanimity. Every moment I remained bonded to Hannah was also a moment I hated. I struggled with the whole situation, rehashing the details endlessly as if somehow that would change them.

One part of my commitment remained constant: I would never leave Hannah just to avoid pain. It would have to feel right, unrushed, peaceful. And peace, at this point, was nowhere to be found.

Most of the people who cared about me kept urging a clean break. There was no coming back from this, they counseled. There was no marriage to save. I dismissed this perspective as simplistic and conventional. What did they know about a love like ours?

My wisest friends gently pointed out that all I ever talked about was Hannah. I kept trying to understand what was indecipherable about her, deluded that cracking Hannah's code would make all the pain go away and convince her to come back. I rarely focused on myself, on what I wanted and needed. My friends saw right through this folly and wished I would, too. But I just couldn't.

Hannah, meanwhile, actually kept trying to come back. She pronounced herself ready on our wedding anniversary—Thanksgiving. We jetted to Amsterdam for a holiday of purported renewal. It began with a huge exhale. Finally, it seemed, the long nightmare was over.

But before we could even find our footing, let alone address the damage, her resolve began to evaporate. The romance of Amsterdam's famed canals was eclipsed by her dark, inward turn. On the plane ride home, a fog of disappointment matched the gray outside our window. By the time we landed at SFO, the whole trip felt like a cruel hoax.

Hannah, it turned out, had no will in the traditional sense. No center. Neither of us had realized it, but somewhere along the way she'd borrowed mine. That worked until careening into Alex revealed her long-festering anger, at me, mostly, for the earlier hurts I'd caused.

Whatever might happen between us in the future, we now agreed, she would have to develop her own center first. So I switched to hoping for that, instead of for any more premature reunions, and steeled myself for a longer haul. While still hating every minute of it.

Not letting go. Round Three.

In the months that followed I lived a stable solo life. I had a great gig as a story consultant in San Francisco. I had free time to write a new screenplay and hopefully climb another rung in Hollywood. I ate well and exercised. I took care of both cats, and came to love them, though I'd never been a pet person before.

At the same time I was still roiled by pain. It was a constant companion, ever portable, leaching my life force like bone broth.

My therapist asked if she could put her hands on my chest. This set off a torrent of grief. Though not a crier, all of a sudden I sobbed uncontrollably. Short of breath, snotty, I mourned not just Hannah but every previous unclaimed loss. It felt profound, satisfying in a way, but also a window into how much more pain was still within.

I didn't recognize it at the time, but this new, direct connection to grief planted another seed for what would later grow into my teaching. Specifically, it demonstrated how "surfing" emotions in the present naturally brings forth waves of the same emotion from the past. Surfing those past waves, too, is how we finally unburden ourselves from them and begin to live in a lighter, clearer way.

On the other side of that first grief wave, it was a little easier for me to hang on.

That's also when my brother and sister-in-law invited me to join them at a rented beach house in Mexico. The first night there, I sipped beer at a plastic table as the two of them prepared dinner. Almost offhand, while she chopped vegetables, Chloe asked how I was doing in the process of getting over Hannah.

I bristled. "What do you mean? That's not what I'm doing!"

Well meaning, she quickly backed off. But the moment stayed with me. Why was I so defensive? Was I really okay with my choice? This not letting go, while simultaneously battling it, had just about run its course.

The next morning I went down to the beach. I bodysurfed, ran, and read. My book at the time was *Pigs in Heaven*, by Barbara Kingsolver. It's all about the families we choose after being battered by those we're given. It brought me back to my earlier proclamation that Hannah was family, chosen family. If that was true, I wondered, why was I so conflicted about waiting for her? Why did I still long for her to be different, faster, better? Why did I consider our suspended animation such an ordeal?

I had no good answer to any of those questions. I let them be for a while. I baked in the sun, drifted into a reverie in which I was temporarily unconstrained by worry or want. In this reverie it occurred to me that beyond mere choice, waiting for Hannah could actually be a privilege. I could view it as rare opportunity to assert my true nature. Not letting go of Hannah wasn't something I had to do—it was who I was!

Soon I emerged, back into the world of worry and want. Amazingly, this new degree of acceptance still held. All traces of fight were gone. I was broken wide open, arms outstretched to embrace life at both its best and worst. Whatever comes, bring it on.

Without pride or premeditation, I had stumbled into what Jon Kabat-Zin calls, in honor of Zorba the Greek, *full catastrophe living*. Ever since, this radical embrace of what life brings, moment by moment, has been one of my touchstones. Along with emotional surfing, it's at the heart of all I teach.

Had I known it back then, I would have sung out the timeless mystical ode:

One to me are fame and shame
praise and blame
loss and gain
pleasure and pain

Hannah's job was complete.
She had destroyed me in the best possible way.
Now I was free.

3

Okay, we're almost there. Almost at the moment, just back from Mexico, when I was perched as usual on my meditation bench and found myself swaying side to side. Almost at the moment when I recognized that something was happening beyond my control or comprehension.

Almost at the moment You woke up in me.

But first, in order to honor Your arrival with the grandeur it deserves, to set the stage for the maddening chaos it wreaked, I have to further contemplate my previous fracturing.

You can wake up, for sure, any damn way You please. People spend their whole lives preparing, but clearly You don't require preparation. Something as accidental as falling off a horse has often done it. How it happens, and to whom, can't be reward or punishment either. Gurus touch hundreds of foreheads at a time with just a feather—administering *Shaktipat*, or the transmission of spiritual energy—and a small portion of adepts fall rapturously to the floor in no discernible pattern. It's tempting to chalk it all up to karma, and to therefore reassert the comfort of an explanation, but let's not do that. Let's allow for the possibility that You sometimes act capriciously, or entirely at random, and that we humans have no idea.

I'm guessing You like it better that way. Wild, savage, Kali and Dionysus all in one.

So take this not as a search for "why," or for the shrinking of Your magnificent mystery into some kind of system, but instead as a final search for what I brought to the dance, for clues about what led to the unique ways we danced together, and still do.

Influence. From the Latin *influere*. To flow in. So much of my life, even before the freeing destruction Hannah unleashed, served to clear the space that would allow such inward flow. Laying waste to the ego's castle, again and again. What I'm trying to say is that maybe the greatest contribution I made to our union, inadvertently, was repeatedly breaking down.

◆

The first great breakdown was physical. In my late twenties I came down with a flu and never fully recovered. I entered the murky, confounding world of Chronic Fatigue Syndrome. I've lived in this world, nonstop, for almost thirty years. At the time of my onset, the diagnosis was widely mocked. Most doctors would just tell patients they were depressed. Since then the syndrome has gained credibility, but there's still no clarity about the cause, or agreement about a better name. Plus, it manifests differently in each person, so there's no uniform way to describe it.

Thankfully, many patients have written compelling chronicles of their experience. One of the best accounts is by Laura Hillenbrand, also the author of the bestseller *Seabiscuit*. I don't have lots to add to this literature myself, and the majority of my symptoms aren't relevant here, but what does matter are the fissures in my psyche caused by coping.

Trying to figure out what was wrong with me, and how to get better, took everything I had. It required that I investigate all approaches, from the most conventional to the most alternative. Along the way I had to correct for the bias of each practitioner. So when a conventional doc made a blanket statement like "homeopathy is just the placebo effect" I had to discard it. Likewise, when an energy healer told me that if her process didn't succeed it was because of my own lack of belief, I had to discard that—and her—too.

I got good at this quickly, all the while crushed by a combination of wrenching exhaustion, digestive distress, whole-body inflammation (which

I took to calling "sand in my veins"), and a previously sharp mind that was now easily overwhelmed and often socked in by fog. The longer my condition persisted, the more willing I was to experiment. At one point, following the advice of an "orthomolecular physician," I injected myself with RNA from sheep.

But nothing ever worked. Each new approach would create a surge of hope, followed by a sucker punch of failure. Over the years I came to see this as the treatment roller coaster, and would often have to disembark for a while so as not to compound the pain.

My illness, similar to the wounded-bird issue, was a problem I couldn't solve. Prior to its onset, I harbored the illusion that my mind was invincible, capable of quickly surmounting any challenge. This hadn't come about by accident. Early assessments, followed by the grave proclamations of parents and teachers, convinced me that anything less than world domination would be due solely to my lack of effort. School was almost always easy, which only served to fuel this hubris. So while other sufferers of my malady might not have taken it so personally, I experienced the arrival of each new symptom as further humiliation.

Without such humiliation, I might have remained a brainy idiot. My inner terrain might have been too full of itself to allow for any intervention, divine or otherwise. In the wake of the illness, I truly grasped the limits of my power. It roughed me up and tilled that terrain until it was sowable.

Practically, this meant living a smaller life. I had to stop short in every endeavor, whether I wanted to or not. Rest was nonnegotiable, while at the same time not restorative. I came to understand that I could either do stuff and feel horrible, or not do stuff and still feel horrible. An hourly Hobson's choice.

As a result of all the downtime, I went in and out of consciousness constantly, fluidly. Sometimes a nap would fully take, other times I would just lie there. The usual boundaries between waking, sleeping, dreaming, and musing got run-down and muddied. Perhaps cross-pollinated.

The most visible change in me, after a few years of illness, was my resignation to it. This compromised, minimized existence was my life now until further notice. Accepting that taught me how to make space in my experience for radical shifts. So when the veils of perception eventually parted during meditation, and my body/mind was invaded by a holy ghost of sorts, I had at least half a chance at peaceful coexistence.

I also came to see, out of necessity, that any symptom had a physical, mental, emotional, and spiritual dimension. I could therefore explore the symptom through any of those dimensions. They all intersected, and would often lead to one another in unpredictable ways. Such journeys always brought me a deeper sense of wholeness, even if I didn't actually get better.

Somewhere along the line I came to see that any life experience, not just symptoms, could be approached the same way. I think this prepared me to embrace the coming mystical encounter in all its forms, and in all its impacts, rather than sorting them into simplistic categories such as blessing or curse.

◆

Another puncture in my self-possession came via political activism. My whole world-saving thing, from an incredibly early age, often took the form of passionate campaigns. In second grade, I wrote and recited an anti-war poem. In sixth grade, I started a neighborhood environmental organization. For my elementary school graduation, I penned the lyrics to a song about nuclear annihilation.

At first I had no living models or mentors for this activism. My Jewish DNA must have had something to do with it, since that religion and culture have always been focused on *tikkun olam*—repairing the world. These attempts continued throughout my adolescence and into early adulthood. I championed the hungry, California's farmworkers, Vietnamese boat people, and the Sandinistas.

In nearly every case, however, my cause was somehow thwarted. The money I raised with bike-a-thons to end world hunger got tangled up in nonprofit bureaucracy. Proposition 14, a farmworker human rights initiative, fell prey to deceptive agribusiness advertising. The boat person I cosponsored to resettle in America didn't actually want to be here. And the Nicaraguan revolution, tragically, collapsed before it had the chance to take hold.

Some of these losses had to do with timing—the majority of my activism took place after the gains of the '60s, against the backdrop of Reagan-era regression. My compadres and I never got to relish a stunning victory like the Civil Rights Act, the end of the Vietnam War, or, much later, marriage equality. My greatest period of political ardor intersected, sadly, with a lull in social progress.

But it wasn't only bad timing. And it wasn't just what happened with the issues themselves, either. The bitterness I felt at each setback had a lot to do with my own grandiosity. I was never one for incremental change, or for the long slog of door knocking and consensus building. I couldn't find solace or credence in the belief that the long arc of history bends toward justice. I wanted change now, because it was right, end of story.

After Proposition 14 lost in 1977, the United Farm Workers Union held a "victory" party. I attended with gritted teeth, and assessed their joy in the struggle as delusional and infuriating. Another decade of similar blows decimated my cockiness and stridency. Did this particular form of abasement, like my illness, help prepare me to consort with gods and demons? It's at least possible.

◆

My travails in the movie business, on the other hand, surely played a part. As far back as I remember, my entire identity was wrapped up in films. My childhood best friend, Mare Winningham, went on to become an Academy Award–nominated actress. Her boyfriend in high school was Val Kilmer. Kevin Spacey (confused, but not yet accused as an abuser) was also in our crowd. Success came early to those three, and I assumed my own triumphs as a writer and director were right around the corner. When that didn't happen I plugged away, making a living as a screenwriter but never fully breaking through.

Hannah and I moved out of Los Angeles in 1993. We found a home in a tiny alternative town in Sonoma County called Sebastopol. At the time I still had a rent-controlled apartment in Santa Monica. I kept it, along with a beat-up old Honda Civic in the driveway, so that no one in the biz had to know I'd left the scene, and so I could still make it to a pitch meeting in about four hours. But those harried and glamorous trips down the coast to fulfill my cinematic destiny didn't materialize, and by our Thanksgiving wedding it was already clear my career was foundering.

When Hannah blindsided me with her affair a year and a half later, I was overweight, depressed, and looking into reactivating my teaching credential. It wasn't just work—my whole place in the world was in question. It seemed inconceivable to exist outside of Hollywood. I wasn't sure I wanted to. And I certainly didn't have a clue where else I might find fulfillment.

So if Hannah's gift of liberation was about reducing my ego to dust, she had plenty of Oscar-caliber help.

◆

Apart from the prompts of illness, pain, and loss, my consciousness has been enthralled with the subject of its own dissolution since before it was even fully formed. In high school I found my way to Dada and surrealism. I was also hit hard by accounts of the Holocaust, which led me to existentialism. Sartre and Camus laid bare the absurdity of clinging to any so-called absolute truth, and in the process piqued my curiosity about other ways to pull apart dominant structures, starting with the self.

A key guide in this exploration was my World Literature teacher, Mrs. F. The daughter of a prominent rabbi, Mrs. F. dutifully took the class and me through the Greeks, the Renaissance—all the usual suspects—but her first love was the Jewish canon. To share that realm, she took me under her wing outside of school, in part because of a not-so-secret wish that I would end up marrying one of her daughters.

At first I wasn't an enthusiastic pupil, because of the stale, rote introduction to the faith I'd previously received at the suburban Sunday school to which my parents sent me. But Mrs. F. would have none of that. She explained that the word "Israel" means "God wrestling," and that any truly alive expression of Judaism meant questioning every aspect of the faith and its teachings.

If I wanted a true taste of my people and their tradition firsthand, she told me, I had to get myself to Israel and study at an orthodox academy called a *yeshiva*. She also told me that if I did take that trip I'd likely never come back. This was a manipulative stroke of genius on her part, because it engendered a headstrong mission in me to go *and* come back, thereby proving her wrong.

The months I spent studying in Jerusalem were intense and rewarding. But, despite all the prescribed and predicted God wrestling that possessed me there, I never came to believe in the Old Testament as divine truth. Without such faith, the whole way of life offered to me at the yeshiva felt beautiful but hollow.

So I did come back home, much to Mrs. F's chagrin. Eventually she forgave me, both for that and for not marrying into her family. We stayed close until her death from cancer two decades later. I'm eternally grateful to Mrs. F. for restoring my appreciation of the awesome gifts of our tribe, even if that appreciation was destined to be mostly secular.

One part of my Jerusalem experience, however, was anything but secular. After our weekly *Shabbat* dinner at the yeshiva, a fellow student invited me to join him at a *tish*. This term is used to describe a wide variety of late-night celebrations among the Chasidic sects that populate the ultra-orthodox section of town, called Mea Sharim.

Getting to the tish meant leaving the familiar and crossing into strange, unknown territory. We found ourselves in almost complete darkness, since no electricity was permitted once the Sabbath began. There were streets leading to alleys, and alleys leading to staircases that rose and fell and wound around one another like a labyrinth. Without my guide, I would never have been able to find our destination, nor to make my way back.

Eventually, we entered a dank concrete basement. It, too, was enshrouded in darkness. Once my eyes acclimated, I saw perhaps a hundred Chasidic men, all in black coats and round fur hats. They were packed shoulder to shoulder. My guide and I nudged our way through the crowd to a sliver of space in which we could observe.

The men were chanting in a guttural drone, eerily similar to the sound produced by monks at a Tibetan monastery. In this case the drone began almost inaudibly, as if born from silence. The volume increased steadily over many minutes. The whole room began to vibrate.

Suddenly I was caught unawares, uplifted by the rising intensity, as if truly airborne. I experienced myself hovering above the crowd, while also still rooted to the ground. Then my body fell away, into formlessness. There was still a sense of a "me" present, but nothing to contain it. I merged effortlessly with everyone present, with the room itself, and especially with the drone as it became nearly deafening.

Then, at an invisible signal, the drone abruptly ceased. Not a single chanter missed the cue. The room, as a result, now pulsed with a radiant silence. I was thrust back into my body, but somehow was also still weightless.

After a few moments, the drone arose softly out of the silence once more. It gradually increased in the same way toward an ear-splitting peak, then stopped all at once. This cycle repeated over and over, for about an hour, before the tish concluded. I filed out of the basement in a mystical reverie, as humbled as I was wobbly.

My reverie in that basement presaged my experience of mirror gazing, twenty years later, as described in chapter 11. More important than that, though, it was an unintended initiation into the *experience* of oneness. I sensed that this oneness—beyond doctrine, tradition, history, or faith—was the true, fiery centerpiece of all Judaism. Later, I also came to sense that this same oneness was also at the center of most other religions. While beliefs among these religions differed widely, a numinous unity was always there for the sharing.

Once home in the United States, I was unable to recapture anything at all like my altered state in that basement. But its echo persisted and increased my curiosity about the nature of consciousness. Specifically, I sought to comprehend any links or portals between mystical union and the everyday, separate-seeming ego.

The beginning of that search took me to Freud, who, famously, broke down that separateness even further by splitting the self into three parts. The way back to oneness, I began to surmise, might counterintuitively begin with fracturing. This supposition was strengthened by my subsequent readings of Fritz Perls. A psychoanalyst who veered from Freud, Perls posited not just three but rather a wide array of sub-personalities unique to each individual. His Gestalt therapy offered a lively set of practices to access that array. This access deepened through the work of Hal Stone and Sidra Winkelman. Their Voice Dialogue process, fortuitously, was the main technique employed by Rebecca, my first psychologist.

Weekly, during my late twenties, I used Voice Dialogue to inhabit different aspects of myself and let them speak freely to the rest of me. One week, for example, I came to therapy frustrated in my love life and a recent series of rejections. I marveled at the way some James Dean types can just lean against a wall, doing and saying nothing, and still rope in women with their effortless sexual charisma. Rebecca asked if I wanted to meet my own internal James Dean. I was shocked, doubtful, titillated.

Rebecca guided me to switch chairs and let him come through. In a seeming miracle, it happened. Though barely knowable, and awkward to inhabit, the sub-personality we called James Dean blinked to life. With the right type of welcome and prodding, he looked, moved, and talked just like one of those real-world wall leaners. As if to make the miracle even more dramatic, Rebecca then gazed at me as if I *were* James Dean, which lit a flame inside me I can still recall to this day.

Is there an actual, discrete, locatable part of my being that's like James Dean? No, just as there's no actual, discrete, locatable being of which my inner James Dean might be a part.

Had I not come to this realization through therapy, Buddhism would have done the trick as well. The Buddhism I encountered in the '70s and '80s came to the West in a new garb, refashioned for our specific tastes and cultural moment. Stripped of superstition, it was distilled to the central assertion that there is no consistent personality at all, not even consistent sub-personalities, but rather an ever-shifting stream of consciousness masquerading as a self, to which everything happens.

On top of all that, one of my early lovers introduced me to deconstruction, the school of literary criticism which challenged the primacy of an authorial vision. Now, not only was it impossible to find a unified self, but any story that such a self might try to tell (this one included!) became equally suspect.

At the time of Hannah's affair and up until my awakening, I worked at Rocket Science Games in San Francisco. Codesigning a graphic adventure about artificial intelligence becoming sentient, I steeped myself in the scientific theory of "hive mind." This term, also known as distributed intelligence, describes how the total knowledge and awareness of a community—in this case bees—is far greater than that possessed by any individual insect.

Hive mind gives lie to the idea of a single, separate, disconnected identity. But rather than getting there by breaking down the self, this school of thought demonstrates how consciousness *exceeds* the self. Opposite direction, same conclusion.

Distributed intelligence is not unique to just a few species. And it spans generations, too. After all, how do the monarchs make their annual trek from Canada to Mexico, arriving at the exact same trees year after year, when it takes as many as five cycles of caterpillar-to-chrysalis-to-butterfly to make the trip?

How do starlings fly in perfect formation without a leader?

It seems likely that what's true about insects and starlings is also true about the human race: a single member can't truly know itself, let alone survive, or even exist, apart from the greater whole.

◆

I didn't study any of this in an ordered or purposeful fashion. It all just came to me, and worked on me, in its own distributed way. Conceptually, like attracted like, and I found myself believing less and less that I was an "I" in the ordinary sense of one. The illusion of myself persisted, and felt real, but it didn't hold up to intellectual scrutiny.

That's why it made total sense to me when neuroscience research began to corroborate this lack of a human self in measurable ways. At this point there are scores of books describing the scientific findings, but one among them stands out for me: *The Mind's Past*, by Michael Gazzaniga. In this very slim bombshell, Gazzaniga describes how the self is a product of evolution, created as a false construct by our own brains. A hand moves before its owner *decides* to move, he tells us, but human perception reverses the order so that it seems—cruel joke!—that we are actually in control.

This not only does a number on the self, but on the entire notion of free will.

Next came the discovery that the digestive system, home of "gut feelings," contains ten times more nonhuman cells than those with our own genetic signature. Science has demoted us from autonomous organism to mere host, a wobbly sack, in which trillions of party crashers forever feed, fight, and fuck. Enterobacter, meet James Dean. Our general well-being is determined by how well all these mental and physical interlopers get along.

Still, the self-illusion is mighty. Not only do we vastly overestimate how much control we have over our lives, we also ignore how much internal functioning happens of its own accord. However it actually gets decided what's for lunch, to take a daily example, we obviously don't know the first thing about how to digest it. Digestion happens to us, not by us.

For me, the most amazing part of all this is that we're not concerned. We don't live in fear that our gut biome, or one of our sub-personalities, will stage a coup and become supreme commander. When the show is working, we take unearned credit for all of it. When it's not, we set about fixing it with whatever approaches and tools are available. But sane people just don't run around screaming that they've been overtaken by foreign forces. I guess that's because it doesn't *feel* that way.

If it did, what would you do?

Here's what I did.

4

We have to resign ourselves.

He's going through with this.

The stage is set.

His credibility has been addressed.

It's time for us to cross our fingers and prepare for the fallout.

What's the worst that can happen?

Too distressing to even think about.

Stomach here—also registering concern.

Biome never queasier.

Not sure we can stop him, but at least we can slow him down.

◆

I hear the chorus of fretting internal selves. I feel the nausea that's made common cause with them. It all gives me pause, but it can't stop me. That's because none of this is led by me, if there even were some kind of fixed me. These words, this whole endeavor, is an outpouring of heart. Ever since waking up began, and especially after the initial upheaval, all mind, all personality, has been harnessed for the heart's mission. This is nothing that happens consciously, or that I could take credit for. With each new breath, each new challenge, the heart leaps to the forefront and offers itself as guide, filter, sounding board, editor. The wisdom of the heart exceeds the self, while paradoxically expressing through it.

Whenever I temporarily veer from love's lead, I become smaller, fallible, unreliable. Whenever I attune to it, I'm still vastly imperfect but always at my best.

One of the fruits of this attunement is my book from 2003, *Setting Your Heart On Fire*. The book begins with this invocation:

Love, speak to me

Render me willing

Receptive

Humble enough to hear your words

Strong enough to live your light

To meet your gaze in all things

To bless them, join them

In your sacred heart of hearts

Amen. Again.

◆

Flying back from the Mexico trip in early 1996, I listened solely to the album *I'm Alive* by Jackson Browne. His *Late for the Sky* was essential to me back in the mid-'70s. He was like an older soul brother, offering me a version of male sensitivity and artistry that I could both cling to and emulate. Over the years I'd moved away from his work. It seemed glued to its time, and also a little earnest for my evolving taste. So I approached this latest album with caution, especially because there were many reports of his bad behavior during a breakup with Darryl Hannah.

I was thrilled, therefore, when it turned out that the album seemed to mirror and celebrate my own recommitment on the beach. It became my anthem for tuning into the pain, for staying strong in that vulnerability, and for choosing to love in spite of everything.

So as the plane landed in the Bay Area, I remained aloft in my sweet sorrow. I returned to my Hannah-less house with a quiet, peaceful trust in whatever was to come.

And then I got sick. The next few days were given over to puking and fever. I'll never know whether it was a standard case of traveler's illness or a prelude for what happened next.

Journal, March 3, 1996:

> As I focus on my breath [in meditation], I begin to hyper-ventilate. The breathing gets deeper, faster, then it becomes a super-fast chugging accompanied by a swaying to and fro and trembling. It fills me up with space inside, and warmth. I feel a band of energy around my throat and neck and all the way up to my ears. Also my shoulders are a part of it. Then the sequence ends with a big, complete breath.
>
> After a few minutes it happens again. This time it feels like a charge is building, starting in my groin and then flowing upward. Then it pauses, and resumes, and in this third wave the charge explodes into great big sobs, and a throaty yowling that I've never made before. After another few minutes the sobs and yowls turn to peals of laughter. The laughter plasters a big smile on my face. It remains, kind of stiff and awkward, until the session comes to an end.
>
> I get up and turn on the stereo. I go to the mirror and watch myself sing "I'm Alive." Resonant. Joyful.

Later I go to my therapist. I tell her about it. She seems concerned. I tell her I'm not reading anything into it. She says it's a sign how big my container has gotten that I can experience and hold and accept all of it.

If I hadn't had any meditation practice at all, I'm sure these phenomena would have been much more alarming. As it was, I'd been meditating for about five years, consistently if not daily, varying from thirty minutes to an hour. At the time my method was Vipassana, or mindfulness.

It was a companion to the meditation I had read about voraciously and tried from many traditions, always with an eye toward the mystical core of these practices.

Over years of watching my internal sensations, I had grown used to the way they came and went, and often morphed rapidly from one to another. What made these new sensations different was how they seemed to be arising from another source. Inside of me, but separate from what I experienced *as* me. Most important, they seemed to have a will of their own.

I related to that will with calm curiosity, and with an undercurrent of grateful excitement.

Journal, March 8, 1996:

> Teeth chattering, head shaking from side to side, tongue wagging, hanging out like the lion pose while I'm producing loud and constant groans. Hands flapping in my lap, entire body tensing and trembling, rigid then releasing.
>
> Sliding off the bench, thrusting my legs over my head into the plow pose. Taking it further, further. Too far. Pulling a shoulder muscle.
>
> Back on the bench. Bouncing up and down. Breathing guttural. Shouting and panting. Like a dog or wolf or infant. Hissing. Extreme facial contortions. Not choosing to do any of this. Just happening.

Later:

> Such a temptation to box all this into something that makes it clear or simple or understandable, and even to try to find other people's writings about it, but I think for now I'll wait.

Each time I sat down on the bench I wondered if it was all over. But almost a week later, it was still going, starting the very moment I sat down, like it was just there beneath the surface, itching to get going.

At that point I was grateful to have remained steadfast in following the Buddha's edict to trust only direct experience. Not once, previously, had I sought out or wished for mystical encounters. I was fascinated by them, but also truly agnostic about their possibility. This made me confident, therefore, that my experience wasn't subconsciously created or incited. It was real. It was happening. To me. I didn't know what to make of it, but I didn't question it either.

Instead, I opened. Over and over. Reveled. Dove into the new channels of electric ecstasy that spread from my chest out to the tips of my limbs. The ecstasy was almost always there, amidst the shock and clamor of the rest. Otherwise, to be honest, I would have been much less welcoming.

◆

Beloved, what was it like for *You* then, in those first moments of our collision? To wake up in a cage of bone and sinew must have felt so disorienting. And the dense, fleshy goo of a human—did it hurt? Did You feel trapped? Was all the breathy body drama about trying to get out? Was is purposeful or just reactive?

In *The Metamorphosis*, by Kafka, a man finds himself inside a bug. An eerie compression, for sure, but nothing compared to a god captive within a man.

I've always understood the All in the One as a theological principle. A divine hologram. But this was literal. The energy of You meeting the matter of me.

I have to offer lots of subjective description for my readers, a personal blow by blow, otherwise it will all just seem hopelessly abstract. But I'm chastened by the risk that brings. I reread my own words from the journal and they often land with a clinical thud. Nothing like the mesmerizing glow and hum You poured through me.

So once again, my apologies—with full understanding if You go dim and silent at these lamentable passages. But is it ever actually true that God (or a god) is in the details? If so, I pray for this be one of those times.

◆

If it seems unhinged or sacrilegious to describe flopping and yowling and buzzing as manifestations from the Almighty, trust me: it's about to get a lot worse.

◆

Journal, March 9, 1996:

> Today, during a round of breathing, my hands begin slapping my head repeatedly, very hard. I throw off my cap and glasses. My hands continue to slap—cheeks, nose, eyes now, too. Wherever they slap, they also scratch. The slapping and scratching broaden to include my chest, stomach, thighs. Up and down my body, sometimes stopping as my arms bend at the elbows and flap like a bird. I feel out of my mind and fully present at the same time. After about ten minutes, all that energy shoots out the top of my head. But its residue is still vibrating within me, even as I type. It's like there's still too much in there. My face is contorting and my tongue is hanging out of my mouth. And Steven is coming over in a few minutes.
>
> [Steven was my design partner at Rocket Science Games. Just out of Harvard, humble and eager, he had one of the most brilliant minds I'd ever encountered. He also had little interest, understanding, or tolerance for "woo." Sharing any of this experience would have been a disaster.]
>
> I get up from my meditation bench and it all continues. This time I start hopping around, slobbering and grunting, as my legs pound faster and faster like that classic football drill. Then

I trip and fall, find myself lying face down on the floor as the slobbering and grunting continue.

I wonder if this will all keep going, like a bad acid trip, but it soon begins to subside. By the time Steven arrives I am able to stay mostly still. One of my legs keeps trembling but I am able to disguise this as mere nervous energy. We get some good work done. I feel happy. After a while my head clouds. I can no longer feel all that energy within me, though I also know it's still there.

Later:

Part of me is getting weary of this, wondering how much I can handle in a day. I have no idea where it's coming from. I'm a little afraid it will end badly or take me somewhere I don't want to go. It almost feels like it has nothing to do with me.

Another part of me is thrilled, considers this a breakthrough, judging mostly by how happy and loose and full it makes me feel. It fits with the little I've read over the years about Kundalini and how it needs to move through the chakras, but that's all I can really say.

It's so weird how I can be talking normally on the phone to someone who has no clue that I'm simultaneously contorted in ways that could get me committed. I need to talk a little about this. Good thing I'm going to see Carol [my chiropractor] tomorrow.

◆

According to Merriam-Webster, Kundalini is "the yogic life force that is held to lie coiled at the base of the spine until it is aroused and sent to the head to trigger enlightenment."

According to *Yoga Journal*:

Kundalini can awaken spontaneously for no obvious reason or be triggered by . . . accidents, near-death experiences, childbirth, emotional trauma . . .

> A spontaneous awakening in one who is unprepared or with-
> out the assistance of a good teacher can result in an experi-
> ence which has been termed as . . . "spiritual emergency" or
> "Kundalini syndrome." The symptoms are said to resemble those
> of Kundalini awakening but are experienced as unpleasant,
> overwhelming, or out of control . . .

At the time I'd heard hardly any of this. Only later would I be able to eval-
uate whether it was the best framework for interpreting my experience.
Or if having such a framework even mattered. But the onslaught of events,
and my need to document them in great detail, gave new life to my most
potent questions:

What does it actually mean to be in control?

Or out of it?

How much of my perceived control is an illusion?

If something brand new and wildly intoxicating and powerful beyond
comprehension begins happening to me, and I choose not to resist and
instead to explore it, does the term "control" even apply?

◆

Journal, March 10, 1996:

> I'm a little worried about how Carol will take all of this—it's not
> in her chiropractic playbook—but she turns out to be accepting
> and sweet. She tells me about a client of hers who wrote a book
> about a similar experience, except her invasion came in the
> form of relentless visions.
>
> [The author is Janet Adler. Her book is *Arching Backward.*]
>
> Back from Carol's and it starts up again. This time my hands
> clasp together ramrod straight above my head, like a classic
> yoga pose, and then they start vibrating, seemingly in search

of something specific. I think to myself, "What do they want to do?"

They land on two points at the base of my head and begin rubbing, pounding, and slapping those points really hard, like trying to shock them into opening. Then my hands move toward my mouth, go inside and start pulling on my upper jaw like craniosacral work. Same thing with my nose. After that my hands seek out my cold feet and begin rubbing and pounding them, too.

I throw off all my clothes and get back on the bench. I feel clearer, quieter. Something is surging through now that seems more raw and essential.

Later:

I notice that my usual exhaustion and this surging energy seem to coexist. Side by side. One doesn't take over the other. I can find myself overflowing with power, and longing to lie down at the same time. Too bad, in a way. I had hoped all this electricity might blast out the Chronic Fatigue Syndrome.

I'm also less concerned than before about this new energy bursting out in public. It feels like a wild animal on a leash. When I take off the leash it bounds freely. When I put the leash back on, it doesn't protest.

But it's always there. In the bath, on my run. All I have to do is focus on it— leash off—and pow!

◆

The term Kundalini means "coiled" and is symbolized by a snake. Most accounts of this energy, once it's awakened, suggest that it moves up the central energetic channels of the body, breaking through and fully activating each of the seven chakras, or energy centers, along the way. One school of thought posits that this process becomes complete when what's known as the crown chakra is fully opened, and the individual can then merge with universal consciousness. Another school of thought considers the process complete when that same energy cascades down the front of the body and takes root in the *hara*, or power center of the solar plexus.

But all of that is like saying the love of a parent for a child is more powerful than any other. It may be true, yet it tells you nothing of what the experience feels like from the inside.

It's that whole "You can't describe the flavor of an orange to somebody who's never tasted one" thing.

Objective or outside truths are essential in certain measurable realms, like blood pressure and moon shots. But when the subject is nothing less than the fundamental powers of the universe, objectivity can play an advisory role at best.

And advice definitely runneth over.

A Google search for "Kundalini" reveals 15,500,000 entries on the topic. The main themes:

- Be careful what you wish for
- It can be blissful
- It can be hell
- Don't get inflated
- Find a reputable teacher
- You may be considered insane

Had such advice been available to me on March 10, 1996, it might have helped at least a little bit. But nothing in all the fifteen-and-a-half million entries would have been of use the next day, March 11.

5

Journal, March 11, 1996:

Yesterday's complacency is gone. I'm scared to death.

This morning I wake up late and plan not to meditate. Figure it's good to skip since I don't want to rev up the big engine with a long workday ahead. Last minute, as I'm crossing the room to leave, a little session spontaneously occurs. A standing one. Hands shoot above my head and there is little to be done but just charge up with it and watch all the energy shoot me skyward and hold me up until a break in the action and chance to fall into regular mode and regroup.

So I do, and hit the road. On the way I'm aware that the charge is right there, and I wonder if it will overtake me. I feel like I can keep it at bay until near the 101 when a few tremors rock my body and a few breaths overtake my calm. I think of the term, "Pull over and pray." I think of the phrase, "Driving under the influence." Only, influence of what?

I get on the freeway and for a while it's just fine—there's two of me. The one driving and the one spilling all over the place. Whenever the spiller bucks my body and tries to take over my breath, I just veto the effort and move on. But then I notice that a few times the energy comes up and is full of a destructive feeling. I shout things, angry things with the force of that energy. I wonder if this is rebuffed energy gone bad or something demonic or just proof that the primal force is filled with equal parts light and dark.

This is a philosophical question until I arrive at the Richmond Bridge. Suddenly the energy inside me is so huge that it needs to escape any and all limitations imposed upon it. Literally, this means that it wants to drive off the bridge. Kill me. I would be dead not out of my own pain or desperation but because something within me needed to get out of me and this was the only way.

[It would be impossible to actually drive off that particular bridge. It would be possible, though, to swerve into the guardrail or other nearby vehicles.]

Needless to say, I freak. Hold onto the steering wheel for dear life. And a shouting match ensues. I shout, "I won't do it!" over and over. And then the other side takes those words and spins them back at me, yelling, in my same voice, "Do it! Do it! Do it!" Then I just find myself shouting at the top of my lungs—no words, just primal screaming.

The rest of the ride is filled with smaller bouts of the same. I finally make it to the office. Before, I'd fantasized about all this joy I'd arrive with, tossing everyone gleeful hellos. Now I'm totally shaken and confused.

The energy keeps sucking me toward it. It takes all my will to resist. The tension is totally exhausting. The underlying buzz is so big, though, that it could overcome me at any moment. I can't spend the whole day like this. I have to find a private place to get some of it out.

I wonder if this is insanity. Forces driving me to do things, making me move, making me unable to function in my daily life—isn't that what being insane is? And yet somehow I still trust this. But maybe it's just too big for me right now. Could I ever turn away from it? How would I even do that? Do I need to try?

Later:

> My computer crashes, so I take the time during reboot to head for the bathroom. I lock myself in a stall. I let it out for a moment. Immediately my hands fly over my head and I begin jumping like a pogo stick. I can tell the energy wants more than ever to get up and out. Problem is, trying to let it out only increases it.

◆

Journal, March 12, 1996:

> After writing the above, I spent the rest of yesterday in and out of the bathroom, using the privacy of the stall to release more of what's within. At one point I assume a new position—bent over frontward with my arms shooting up behind me. Like I'm about to leap into the air and take off.
>
> At the end of the day I call Hannah. [We're about nine months into our first separation at this point, but still in close contact.]
>
> Without prompting, she uses the words "Kundalini experience." Careful not to label further, Hannah suggests I talk to Theresa, an esoteric healer we both trust. Hannah also says, "We know one thing for sure. This energy is not all good. It tried to get you to drive off a bridge."
>
> I haven't wanted to face that because the adventure has felt so important, like a privilege. Hannah thinks I should say very little to Theresa and see what she picks up on. Luckily she's available, and I'm driving to her place tomorrow afternoon.
>
> Last night, home from work, a sexual component of the energy burst through. It was always there before, in the background, but at this point it just takes over. I watch myself go through multiple rounds of desire and stimulation, noticing that none of it is actually pleasurable. The sexual energy feels like a tool for opening me up, clearing me out, making room for more.

This morning, I wake up to more of the sexually charged energy. Soon I'm shuddering with it, and then in a new twist my hand flies up to my throat as if to choke me. I can't tell if this has anything to do with the whole opening process. It's not actual choking because the force isn't that strong and it's clear I can stop it at any time. Maybe it's a way to build up pressure, in order to intensify the surges that follow.

Then the same hand moves over my mouth and covers it as if to suffocate me. Again, not for real because I can breathe just fine, but some kind of symbolic suffocating, just like the whole driving-off-the-bridge thing was symbolic.

Now here I am, grateful that my appointment with Theresa is soon. Because this whole ride is so fraught now, even as it still thrills me.

Later:

Hannah suggested that I keep my eyes open and try to stay in my body when the energy gets strong. I tried, in a second round after the choking and suffocating, and it went like this:

I slide off the bench and round forward like I'm about to go into a headstand. Using the ottoman in front of me for support, I settle into a shoulder stand instead. My feet rocket straight up and begin to tremble and shudder like my hands usually do. After a few minutes of this I'm taken backward into the plow position again, like on that first day.

I take the plow further than usually possible, to where I used to be able to get to about fifteen years ago. The plow continues along with the shuddering and, now, wild breathing. I rock back further and further, legs straightening, flexing, smacking the floor . . . until I pull another muscle, this time way worse.

Angry, I shut off the energy and walk around, assessing the extent of the injury. I won't be able to play basketball tonight. Who knows if I'll be able to sit in the dentist's chair tomorrow morning. That's two pulls in one week. The pain is still really bad as I type this. There's a cold pack wrapped around my midsection.

It feels like the energy is intent on taking me past my physical limits, but without discretion or clear purpose. While I'm still trying to do regular life!

Time for more ibuprofen.

◆

Months afterward I would learn of a Hindu legend that asserted the hatha yoga asanas were developed by watching people during spontaneous Kundalini awakenings. These people would thrust themselves into the now-familiar postures with bodies most certainly better able to hold them than mine.

Current scholarship doesn't attach much credence to this legend. Personally, painfully, I'd guess that it's true.

◆

After lying in the dentist's chair with my back on fire, I headed up the mountain to Occidental. Theresa, about forty, lived by herself in a remote cabin. Silver-gray hair flowed to her waist in ringlets. She chewed anise seeds and smelled like licorice. She was lighthearted, but also exuded a natural spiritual authority. A young crone.

Theresa had recently worked in Hannah's acupuncture office as a massage therapist and energy healer. I had loved getting her treatments and found the impact of no-touch sessions far more powerful than hands on. Prior to walking through her door that day, I had no idea of her background or training. Later I learned that in addition to her intuitive skills, Theresa had apprenticed in both Tibetan medicine and the Healing Light Center of Rosalyn Bruyere.

Journal, March 13, 1996:

I trust Theresa without hesitation. From the grave look in her eyes I can tell that she takes me seriously and senses great danger.

I lie down on the table in her treatment room. She asks me to tell her everything, so I cast aside Hannah's suggestion not to say much and instead launch in. I split the account into three parts, the mild beginning, the intense middle, and the scary now. When I'm done, Theresa asks if I am willing to part with any of this energy that means me harm. I say yes. She makes it clear that once we're done with our work, it might be gone altogether. Do I accept that? Yes. Though I don't know what is to come, I do know there is no other choice.

Theresa leaves the room for a moment and returns with sage, a feather, tissues, and some bells. I sense this is meant to be an exorcism of some kind. I don't believe in that term and associate it with Linda Blair, spinning heads, and special effects vomit. Yet here I am.

Before she sets about confronting this energy directly, I want her to see and experience it. So with her okay I let some through, minding my injured back the whole time. This version includes a huge smacking of my third eye, over and over. Theresa tells me that one important sign that an energy is harmful is that it treats the body harshly, unkindly. She says that a beneficent energy would always be gentle and patient.

[Though my subsequent experience taught me that this guideline is not always true, it served me well to heed her at the time.]

Theresa burns some sage. She instructs me to be totally present in my body, and to begin to resist the energy. She asks me to breathe in my own way, into my belly. She invokes the deities to help me rid my body of any presences that don't mean me well. She claims my body for the light, for the good.

The energy has other ideas. It begins to get huge, and defiant.

Theresa implores me to keep resisting the power and stay in my body. "I can't, I can't," I reply in a very small voice. "It's too big." She keeps speaking sternly to me and the power, but all I can do is let it overtake my legs and head and anything else it wants. I keep breathing the way she asks, but the power only grows stronger.

Theresa asks the power to speak. I am there for this, but also gone as it hollers, "NOOOOOOOOOOOOOOOOOOOOO!"

Theresa asks its name. It yells, "I AM!"

Then a dialogue begins. Theresa invokes more of the light and the good, and in response, the power taunts her. They go a few rounds this way. The power alternates between fever pitch and eerily soft. I remember only snippets of its words.

"He's mine . . . You don't know . . . He dies . . . He is dead . . . He came to me . . . He belongs to me . . . He . . . belongs . . . to me."

Theresa attacks this directly, refuting every point. Then it barrages her with lots of foul name-calling.

Theresa speaks to me again, asking me once more to claim my body and send the power away. I'm trembling, sobbing, unable. I can repeat her words softly, and even with some conviction, but I'm not strong enough to cast the power out. I don't want to surrender to its evil, I just want to quit fighting. And, in truth, I don't want to let go of the positive part of what I'd encountered.

Then comes the beginning of the turning. Theresa asks me to see that the positive part I want to hold onto is linked to the evil we'd both just witnessed. I see that. She asks me to look for and cling to anything in me that is good. I cry and cry because I want to but can't. The best I can do is confirm that I don't want to die. But that isn't enough.

The energy is mostly in my hands now, and I can feel it wanting to reach out and strangle Theresa. It comes close. In that moment I know it could kill. I know this energy is truly out to destroy.

Suddenly, I see a vision of myself killing Hannah. I know that if I don't find the strength to resist and cast this energy out, she, too—whom I love more than anything on earth—would be at grave risk.

That is it. It's all over. There is no chance in hell that I would ever harm her.

There would still be much more to come, but the end was now a foregone conclusion. The power would have to go, and I would have to find the strength to let it.

◆

Journal, March 13, 1996, continued:

> Toward the end of her ministrations, when I have sufficiently reclaimed my inner space, Theresa invokes the name of archangel Raphael. That strikes me deeply, because for years I have wanted to replace my given first name, Howard, with one of my given Hebrew names, Raphael.
>
> Theresa doesn't know that until I tell her. I explain that I love its meaning, "God heals" or "healed by God." She tells me that she usually speaks his name last during invocations, but this time it just seemed right to put him first. For me, the meaning of the name is finally beginning to apply.
>
> Before sending me off, Theresa admonishes me to stay strong and vigilant, to keep rebuilding my "field of protection." She asks me to invoke whatever god suits me. Strangely, shockingly, all I can think about is Jesus. Not the Jesus of religion, or the reputed messiah, but Jesus the fount of compassion. Instead of going with a more general invocation like, "Help me, God," what I really want to say is "Help me, Jesus."

Born and raised Jewish, educated to be on guard against all attempts at conversion, and to see Christians as both an historical and present-day threat, this yearning was a lot to accept. But I did try, just as I tried to accept this entire unbelievable experience.

◆

Journal, March 13, 1996, continued:

> Heading home, I feel like an addict with a drink in my hand. That's how close the energy still is. One momentary lapse, one false breath, and I'd be right back where I was before. It worries me that after the exorcism I could still be in danger, but I know it without a doubt.
>
> I continue to ask for protection, and to summon a vision of Hannah, still very much alive, in order not to give in to the energetic lure.
>
> Once I reach my house, the lure abates a little. I smudge the whole place and take a soothing bath. During the bath I feel a wave of sorrow and emptiness, having just slammed the door on all the amazement and drama. Without the electric bliss, without the mortal enemy to vanquish, all I have left is the misery of the last nine Hannah-less months.
>
> I take Theresa up on her offer to be available by phone. I share the sorrow and emptiness with her. Talking about it lessens the pain. After we hang up I pray again, this time not just for protection but also, if possible, to find a similar power from a beneficent source.

◆

Before that day, my worldview didn't include the possibility that nonphysical energy, from a supernatural source, could take up residence in a human body, without asking for or receiving consent, and set about fulfilling its own mission.

Before that day, my worldview didn't include the possibility that nonphysical energy, from a supernatural source, could take up residence in a human body, with malicious intent to victimize its host.

Before that day, my worldview didn't include the possibility that deities, such as Jesus, could be enlisted for protection from malicious energy.

Before that day, I didn't believe that such things were even *possible*, let alone that they could happen to me. Then they did. But I still questioned the story, and still do, regardless of my detailed journal entries from the time. For example, despite all my insistence that these entities operated outside my personal will, is it possible that they were aspects of my unconscious, split off into seeming separateness because I wasn't yet able to integrate them into my conscious self?

Here's some fuel for that perspective. During the preceding nine months of Hannah hell, I almost never got angry at her. Mostly I found myself migrating toward compassion for all the turmoil she was clearly undergoing. Some might say that's abnormal, unhealthy, and that if I wasn't accessing my anger directly then it would need to find another outlet. So could what Theresa and I both saw as a demonic invasion actually have been my own rage, fortified by denial to the point that it turned potentially murderous?

I can't say. All I can say is that it didn't feel like that then, and it doesn't now.

What about the possibility that all the emotional pain I'd been through led to a temporary psychosis? Had Theresa perhaps enabled that psychosis rather than addressed it?

For this answer I defer to Bonnie Greenwell, a psychologist who has perhaps done more research on the Kundalini phenomenon than anyone. Greenwell suggests that people with serious mental illness are uniformly unable to describe their experience rationally while it's happening. In my case, during the most overwhelming Kundalini explosions, not to mention during full-blown demonic possession, I was always able to narrate clearly.

Short of a complete mental breakdown, perhaps there's a case for a kind of soul confusion, or what my mentor Martin, referenced earlier, called a "spiritual Disneyland." Could the whole incredibly specific tableau be a manifestation of the tension between some inexplicable elemental energy that needed to push through me—Kundalini or otherwise—and all the places in my psyche where it just couldn't penetrate? Isn't that foretold somewhat, as I alluded to earlier, in the idea of karmic knots and the kriyas they often cause?

If this diagnosis were correct, then all of the confounding details of my story wouldn't matter. They'd be mere side effects or by-products. Of the possible explanations that might render my experience illusory, unreliable, or insignificant, this one seems to have the most potential.

But as the events to come will demonstrate, there's no easy way to fully separate actual awakening from the chaos that often surrounds it. In my case, anyway, they seemed at the outset to go hand in hand. One might not have been possible without the other. A fully stabilized heart opening, perhaps, required this preliminary battle.

If for that reason alone, I'm compelled to keep sharing more.

◆

Journal, March 14, 1996:

> After hanging up with Theresa I head for bed, scared that in sleep my guard will be lowered. It isn't. I wake up with worse back pain but feeling safer. I also feel wobbly, disoriented, with the recognition that my life has been forever altered. How it happened, and why, will surely take a long time to crystallize. I vow to stay as present as possible. I have no clue what will happen next.

> All morning I can feel the terrifying energy right there, inside me, just waiting for a moment to be set free. I keep my guard up constantly, with great effort. Whenever I feel the tingle, the pull, I clamp down with everything I have.

> Around noon I actually go to work. At times, like during meetings, the whole turmoil drifts far away. Then, once I'm alone, I feel it right there again and summon my block. One time I look for it and find nothing. I wonder if it has gone away, is behind

me, or perhaps never really happened at all. So I purposely open the door a crack and find it strong as ever, ready to pounce.

The next day, still vigilant, I go back to Theresa. I don't know what she'll advise—another exorcism? Something altogether different? After I fill her in, she asks me to lie down so she can work with my body and energy. As she does, I become confused about what it means to keep my guard up. If all this is happening within, if the demonic energy itself is within, then isn't all of "within" already contaminated? And if so, how can I tune into and trust my own native energy?

Theresa responds that this struggle is indeed occurring on an inner plane, but not one that lines up with an understanding of "within" that is physical or spatial. She says that this inner plane also doesn't correlate with the impersonal, undifferentiated state that gets tapped via meditation. Surrendering to that, at this point, would only place me at greater risk.

To win this battle once and for all, Theresa instructs, I have to learn how to find the right reinforcements. While I continue to lie on the table, she begins to summon deities from an array of spiritual traditions. She names them one by one. Some I've heard of—Vishnu, Tara—and others are completely unfamiliar. As Theresa proceeds, I feel a great longing in my heart for Jesus. Again. I almost begin to cry, wanting to shout out, "Say Jesus! Why aren't you saying Jesus?!" She doesn't, and eventually I ask her to.

Theresa explains that she hasn't invoked Jesus until now out of deference to my Jewish roots. Once she goes ahead and invokes him, I feel the reinforcements cohere with much greater intensity. The demonic energy lessens. I feel brighter, gentler.

Then, suddenly, I am suffused with a loving light, or force, unlike anything I've ever known.

Once again my being is completely overtaken, but this time I trust it without reservation. I just know I can.

My arms and legs shoot straight out into a cross. My heart wells. I am suspended in a love that is both gentler and stronger, by far, than the demonic power.

Of their own volition, my hands rise up and clasp together. I shake, sob. My breath deepens and I assume a whole new set of positions. All the while, Theresa keeps assisting the process, hands on, responding to each new shift.

All of this is very close to what occurred during the demonic spell, but now it is purely sweet, not scary or harmful at all.

As this goes on, I begin to have a much more personal-seeming relationship with this power I need to call Jesus. The need is strong enough to blow away everything in my cultural and genetic identity that would preclude it. Even strong enough to blow away my shock at its presence. I feel no shock, or even surprise. Just a profound clarity that a loving power is saving me.

During this time words come out of my mouth that I never would have uttered previously, and that I am not consciously choosing to say. I hear myself proclaiming, "Jesus loves me" over and over. I hear myself say, "Jesus is my savior." At the end of this recitation I hear myself saying, "Jesus is my father."

My hands reach out and embrace Theresa. When the embrace ends, one hand remains lovingly, affirmingly on her back. It is my hand but it isn't my hand. And part of the feeling that flows through it is sensual. I feel an overpowering urge to do something that I can barely allow. I fight it, and then I can't.

I say to Theresa, "There's something I need to do that's scary, but I have to do it." I take her hand, the one that was on my belly, and lift it in the air about a foot above my groin. I don't know what will happen, or what this means, except that I want the sensual part of me included with everything else that's happening. And so it is, quietly, no big deal. She keeps her hand there for a minute or so, and I just feel more whole, more enveloped. Then she moves on without speaking of it, and I do, too.

The rest of the experience is a bliss so stunning that I never want it to leave. It is like the loving light has a weight and a body of its own and wraps me inside it. Theresa makes it clear to me that I can call on this energy at any time, and that I need a surefire way to do that. So I look for the right words to invoke. Many roll by. None feel right. So I wait, as my limbs continue to undulate.

Then the right words come through with sharp clarity: "Jesus come." The connotation of divine sexual union matches exactly how I feel. Pure, free, united, ecstatic. Theresa shows me some statues of the same kind of union represented in Tibetan spiritual art.

Jesus come. That is my call if and whenever the other power threatens to overtake me. As the ecstasy fades just a bit, Theresa asks if there is anything else that needs to be said. I hear myself saying to her, as an emissary, "You are good. You are love. You are ours."

◆

Right in the middle of that monumental experience, even at the very moment I felt myself being saved by the divine loving force of Jesus, a separate stream of thought also ran through my mind. I wondered, in a kind of play-by-play analysis, if now I was going to have to convert to Christianity. Would I soon become a card-carrying member of Jews for Jesus?

This query, as soon as I became aware of it, struck me as hilarious. I knew at the very deepest level that this force required absolutely nothing of me. It didn't pertain to or entangle itself with the realm of human choice at all. As a result, conversion wasn't even on the table. But thankfully, amidst this gravest battle between darkness and light, there was still room for a wisp of humor.

6

Okay, looks like we're through the worst of it:
an invading will,
freakish energies,
wild contortions,
primal roars,
inexplicable bliss,
demonic possession,
fantastical exorcism,
heavenly salvation.

Anything left out? Anyone want to weigh in?
Stomach here—eerily settled.
Approval seeker here—guess I just stopped caring.
Image protector here—somehow I'm okay with the mess.
Heart here—thank you all so much for your tolerance during this trying time.

Anyone else? Should we even attempt to bring in the Wildness?
Left brain here—that's an adamant no. It never follows the rules. It never plays nice. I mean, it would be one thing if it showed up as even remotely relatable. Like with St. Francis. Or Jill Bolte Taylor. But the truth is, even after all this time, it's often almost indistinguishable from the original Demon.

Sorry, left brain. All good points, but I'm afraid you're too late. My very mention of the Wild One piqued its interest. It's here. Blasting down the door. All we can do now is wait.

◆

Pay your bills

Your taxes, too

I'm coming for you

That ache in your hip

Your busy schedule

Ha!

I'm not just knocking from the inside

I'm razing it to the ground

Till there's no ground

Thoughtful points of view

Your reputation

Who are you kidding?

Not some magic mushroom

Not even the shit it grows in

I'm Love's war paint

If you're not dancing

You're deserting

And I take that personally

"No man shall see my face and live"—

So old school

See me! I need that!

I've commandeered your tongue

Your hips are weightless, ache-less

Lapping in my seas

Don't ask why

Just lick the holy water

And thank me

◆

Okay, that was a lot.
I can see you're all dazed.
But at least we're still intact, right?
Let's all just get some rest.

◆

Journal, March 16, 1996:

I think I get it now. Energy is just energy. So when I encountered the demon, the demon wasn't the energy. The demon somehow attached to the energy and rode in on it. (In Mexico? After?) And even if the demon did bring the energy, it doesn't belong to him. Just like it doesn't belong to Jesus. Energy is energy.

It just is.

What this means to me is that I always have the power to orient the energy, with help and protection, toward the light. As I write this it sounds like some kind of sermon, but I actually mean it in a very practical way.

I checked in with Theresa about this yesterday. She told me, "When the dense inky energy of the demonic presence was replaced by the warm golden energy of the light presence, there was no net loss of energy."

Okay, so we're clear on that.

She said that somehow in my bid for power, I needed to be tested. And the passing of this test has led me to where I am now. She said that I am very blessed to have made it through all these passages so quickly, in particular the turn toward the light. She said the gift of ecstasy is in no way an easy experience. If I don't want it I can still send it away, but sending it away after awakening has occurred is much harder than defeating the demonic.

Well . . . I don't remember making any bid for power. And I don't want to send the ecstasy away. But the surges keep coming with more and more strength.

Theresa told me that in many indigenous cultures not only would all this be understood, but I would also be taken care of while going through it. That makes sense, because what I really need is to take a break from work, have someone else do the shopping, cooking, cleaning, and use the freed-up time and space to let everything settle.

Right now it's definitely not settled. Many of the same roars and writhings that troubled me so much during the demonic time are still occurring, only now just softened a bit in the presence of Jesus. I've wondered a few times whether I was actually safe, and not just deluding myself, but things really are different, and I really am okay. I mean, rubbing my third eye is a lot different than smacking the hell out of it.

But still, I feel like there's a war for the energy in me. Each time it comes up is a new battle. I take the right side. We always win, if winning means I'm not in danger of harm or possession, but at the same time I'm still confused and exhausted.

Theresa described the war this way: "We all live in heaven, and we all live in hell, and we all live here on earth . . . all at the same time."

I'm not sure what that really means, but somehow it rings true.

At the end of the most recent battle, it got sexual. What came into my mind's eye was a kind of earth mother, spread out and beckoning on the ground, taking her form from the trees and grass and hills. Instead of "Jesus come," this time it was, "Love me, mother." And she did. And we did. It felt perfectly natural that the earth was my mother and that we were lovers.

Theresa told me that she felt the mother there, too, during our sessions, and that I can call on that energy as well. She paused, waiting for words, and then said that I can climb into the lap of the mother and even suckle at her breast. Then she said, "Yes, thank you," to whatever had given her those words. It felt strange to hear her talking that way, as she had a few times before, even after all that had been spoken through me.

Later:

The energy just blasted through me so intensely that I had to take a break.

Following Theresa's advice, during the worst of it, I curled up on my bed as if in the mother's lap. It felt good. I found my thumb going into my mouth. I never sucked my thumb as a child, but now I did it easily, rhythmically, rocking back and forth.

After a few minutes I was overcome by a need to be outside. I hurried to the yard and lay down in the wet grass and cool mud. It felt good to be there as well. Another version of the lap.

Soon, though, I was beset by insatiable hunger. I ate a half loaf of bread in one sitting. It's only been about ten minutes since then and I'm still ravenous for the other half.

Is this some kind of grounding, or fuel for more spirit war?

Energy is energy. Ecstasy is ecstasy. But what if it's too much?

◆

The singular power of Jesus faded for me over the years, but never left. Therefore, it feels vital to double back to it one final time. I never did have the desire to commune with Christians, or to get involved with what Theresa called "Churchianity." But as I wrote in another journal passage, Jesus seemed to have "a direct line to my heart. Only by saying his name does my heart open in a full way."

I came to refer to the experience with the term "Christ Consciousness," rather than Jesus, because it felt more like an oceanic love than something that could be tied to a specific being of any sort. It also had nothing at all to do with belief. Christ Consciousness was and is for me a kind of channel on the dial of existence, one that blessedly broke through my personal static and became available ever after. All I have to do to access it is tune in.

That's why, about eight years later, when I began giving presentations at Unity churches throughout the United States, nothing about the experience felt alien or uncomfortable. Of course it helped that the Unity movement is nondenominational and welcomes people of all spiritual paths.

That's also why it didn't surprise me to learn, some time after my experiences with Theresa, that the Kundalini literature is filled with people experiencing direct, full-blown visitations from deities outside their birth traditions.

Does this somehow mean that the deities are real, in the sense that we usually apply that term? I don't think so. Instead, to me, it seems to point toward a nonphysical field of connection that we all emerge from and are never separate from. At extreme moments, that field may cause us to traverse time, space, history, and culture. Suddenly we're "here," and also "there." Multi-local, so to speak. Such multi-locality could enable a human version of what Einstein referred to as "spooky action at a distance."

In physics, the field of connection under study is that which causes objects that were once linked at the dawn of the universe to affect one another across light years. In the case of human beings, it seems that the same field expresses as what psychoanalysis pioneer Carl Jung called the collective unconscious. This is also what psychologist M. Scott Peck, author of *The Road Less Traveled*, was pointing to when he posited that the unconscious itself is God. Without going that far, I'm suggesting that the collective unconscious is

vehicle through which aspects of the divine, or source energy, can
themselves for human perception (more about that in chapter 10).

If the divine is infinite, then might it offer itself in a multitude of
forms through many cultures? And since all those forms are expressions of
the same source, might we sometimes receive temporary dispensation for
direct encounters with new, exotic gods?

It's often said that all the world's religions offer different paths to the
same truth. This perspective can be misleading because religions are human
institutions that offer widely differing cosmologies and precepts. They are
probably more different than they are alike. On the other hand, as I first
intuited during my visit to the tish in Jerusalem, it might be accurate to say
that the fiery mystical center out of which most religions were fashioned *is*
one and the same. It is to me, now, whichever god patches me in.

◆

Over the next couple weeks I felt less wracked by the struggle between
darkness and light. The emanations of that struggle were still present, but
shifted to the background. In the foreground was the energy itself, and the
new pressing questions that came with it.

What is the energy's purpose?

Is it safe?

Do I have a say in how it manifests?

If so, how can I assert that?

Even though I didn't feel that my life was in danger, the energy was
demanding more time and attention. It was also growing in strength and
manipulating me in new ways. I did my best to remain a neutral witness and
compliant subject, sensing, or at least hoping, that this was the right approach.

The energy functioned in a dual way. First, it created experiences
within me. Another word for this might be symptoms (as referenced earlier regarding "Kundalini Syndrome"), and it might be applied here in the

way we speak conventionally about a headache or restless legs. But to label something a symptom also suggests there's an illness or physical problem associated with it. Nothing coming from the energy felt like that (yet). Nor did it feel like the source of these experiences was my own body/mind.

My own body/mind, the "me" I knew, and which I had been expanding in so many ways for so many years already, seemed relegated in this case to a mere conduit.

The second way the energy functioned was as a "doer," animating my body/mind within and without at its own behest. In any journal entry about limbs moving, sounds forming, or actions being taken, it was always the energy that was choosing it to occur and then making it happen. My "me" always had the option to allow or resist, but as a reaction only to what was already underway. I couldn't prevent something before it happened, or turn it off fully once it began.

A separate-seeming life force was now sharing the space of my body/mind. We were roommates, so to speak. As a roommate, the energy was inconsiderate, unruly, and uncooperative. If there were any guidelines or protocols to be had, those would need to come from me.

Rereading that description, it seems like I was sharing a cell with a sociopath. But the feeling that accompanied this arrangement was never like that. It felt absolutely necessary, even a privilege, which is why I continued to make more space for it.

This effort didn't mean shrinking my own portion of the space, but rather clearing and enlarging the whole space we both occupied. This could only work as a joint project. My job was to forgive all the boorishness and let the mysterious portal remain open. The energy's job was radical demolition.

Here are two representative examples of the joint project from that time.

Journal, March 26, 1996:

> I'm on my knees. My hands are pressed together at my heart, in the bowing posture. I bend over till my forehead is pressed

against the floor. I alternate between charging breaths and loud, sustained tones. In the middle of this, my hands go to my ears and pull the flaps tight as possible over the openings. My mouth clamps shut, too, even as the toning continues. It seems like all that vibration locked inside my head is meant to rock something free.

Next I find myself drooling into my hand, wondering what the moisture is for and where it will be applied. Turns out it's my nose. I get it thoroughly wet, inside and out, and then clamp that shut, too.

This demolition continued day after day, sometimes for hours at a time. As more space opened up, both physically and spiritually, the energy became able to express a psychic power as well. The entry that follows describes the first time that the energy knew something about the world outside us that I didn't.

I'm driving on the 101. I feel something like hunger, but not exactly. More like the energy is hungry. My hand begins to tremble, sort of like a zombie. It reaches behind the driver's seat. I think that space is empty. But suddenly my fingers wrap themselves around a bag of rice cakes that must have rolled there during a sharp turn. My still-trembling hand retrieves the rice cakes from the back seat, unseals the package, and presents a crumbly cake to my mouth.

It may seem dangerous, or even approaching suicidal, to be driving seventy miles per hour on the highway while simultaneously letting the energy rip. After all, this is the same energy that, when hijacked just a couple of weeks earlier by a demon, tried to run me off the Richmond Bridge.

I get that. Completely. Which is why it's important to stress how quickly the whole body/mind sharing phenomenon began to feel commonplace. Parts of me were still always wary, for sure, but the majority of me somehow knew that I was fundamentally safe.

Until I wasn't. There would be many times over the next year when the joint project went awry, when I truly was just a split second from catastrophe. But the greatest reassurance that I now had, post-exorcism, and with the mediating power of Christ Consciousness, was the ability to determine the difference between that which was bewildering yet benign, and that which could actually cost me my life.

This new normal set in so quickly, and so securely, that in another part of the above journal entry I noted how at times the entire energetic spectacle, while still increasing in both intensity and strangeness, was sometimes actually a little boring.

◆

Another reason for my driving on the highway was work. I was still going into Rocket Science a few days a week. It felt important to keep a semblance of routine, and worldly engagement, while the joint project continued. I also let on nothing to my coworkers. I knew they would just be terrified, both of me and for me. I had no way to talk about my experience that would be remotely comprehensible to anyone but Hannah and Theresa. And my friend and mentor, Martin, was out of the country on retreat and unreachable.

Luckily, the building that housed Rocket Science had an accessible roof. There was constant construction in the area, too, especially because the new San Francisco Giants baseball stadium was going up just a block away. Whenever the energy would back up, grow too strong, or for any other reason need an outlet, I'd find an excuse to take my leave. Once on the roof, I could stomp and shake and gesticulate without fear of discovery. I could also shout and chant and tone at the top of my lungs, since even the most piercing sound would get lost in the cacophony below.

In between roof visits, though, I still needed to contend with the whole range of smaller tremors and urges. I quickly became adept at disguising the energy's insistence as something more ordinary, like a yoga stretch. Most of the time this would do the trick.

One exception occurred during a scoring session for our game, *Obsidian*, with the well-known tech composer, Thomas Dolby ("She Blinded Me with Science"). There were five of us in a cramped room, and the energy became focused on my mid-back. That was a spot I'd already been working with for many years. It first came to my attention in 1979 when I couldn't achieve a straight spine in my modern dance classes at UCLA.

My orthopedist at the time took an x-ray and announced that three of my vertebrae were fused and that nothing could be done. I took the x-ray to a chiropractor for a second opinion. He suggested that the vertebrae were wedged, not fused, and that my slight hunchback, or kyphosis, might very well respond to intensive therapy.

When I undertook that therapy, the vertebrae didn't really shift. But that whole area of my back came alive with what felt like constant electricity. Plus, I felt an irresistible compulsion to stretch, to pry apart the vertebrae from all angles, using anything at hand. The headrest of my car was the most frequent item, which meant that I would often drive while in simultaneous, self-induced traction.

This, it turns out, was an earlier version of my driving under an energetic influence, as well as an earlier version of a powerful force awakening within me. In these earlier versions, however, the whole thing felt solely neuromuscular, and all "me." Nothing foreign about them, despite the eerie foreshadowing.

After about six months of dealing with this mid-back mega voltage, things quieted. But I also fell into a pattern in which every few weeks the entire area would seize up into an excruciating, burning ball. It would require ninety minutes of intense stretching, followed by a day of post-stretching soreness, for the area to once again even out. Years later I learned a series of gentler, shorter daily exercises that kept things open enough to avoid the previous cycle of seizing.

But now, here I was with Thomas Dolby and my coworkers. There was barely enough room for me to turn around. Right at this point is when the energy decided that it, too, needed to mess with my vertebral wedge. It switched the area on, sent in a jangly, disturbing charge, and yanked at my fascia with a force I could barely tolerate.

For a while I was able to pass off my predicament as ordinary stiffness. I employed my go-to set of nonthreatening yoga postures. After an hour or so, however, my contortions grew unavoidably more bizarre and the dirty looks started coming. Still, I couldn't help it. Soon there was audible snickering. There might even have been a "Dude, what the hell?" I did my best to deflect this all with humor. It was a blessing, as the irritation with me crested, that the team decided to break for lunch.

◆

With Martin still away, and Theresa on standby, it seemed like a good time to look for additional support. My first call was to the Kundalini Yoga Center in Oakland. I figured that they would be experts in how best to deal with the energy, especially since now it was no longer intertwined with separate, nefarious forces.

Amazingly, the woman I spoke to at the center had nothing to offer. She said that the entire focus of the Kundalini yoga movement was to prepare the body for the easiest possible passage of the energy if it happens to awaken. Once it does, more or less, you're on your own.

Next, I focused on the intense breathing that always came with the energy. Somewhere along the line I'd learned about Stanislav Grof and his Holotropic Breathwork. Grof, a prominent early researcher into the transformative properties of LSD, found that certain intensified breathing patterns could produce similar effects. It just so happened that Grof and one of my favorite Buddhist teachers, Jack Kornfield, were about to hold their annual joint retreat.

Since dropping into presence was no longer silent or still for me, but rather an invitation for the energy to go wild, I wondered whether there still might be a way for me to participate. I called the retreat's registration line and asked. The answer was no.

There was still one more way, however, that I might benefit from Grof's work. He and his wife Christina had seen a need for special guidance during what they termed "spiritual emergency." They had written a seminal book about the topic called *The Stormy Search for Self.* Following the book's publication they had also created the Spiritual Emergence Network (SEN), an organization that provided training and accreditation for healing professionals.

I got my hands on a list of SEN-trained supporters and called two in my area. The first one offered platitudes about how the Kundalini awakening experience, though rocky, was ultimately for the best. She had no experience with it directly, and got on the list after attending just one weekend workshop. Instinctively, I knew we weren't a match.

The second accredited counselor I called responded to my voice mail with one of her own. "Soooooooo, you're having a Kundalini crisis," she began, in a tone that was a disconcerting combination of entertained and salacious. "I'd love to roll up my sleeves and get into that with you." Again, not a match. I gathered that while SEN may be a lifeline for others, my path led elsewhere.

But where, exactly? In the midst of my uncertainty I remembered Rebecca, the therapist who had introduced me to my inner James Dean. Rebecca drew upon a fascinating combination of influences beyond just Voice Dialogue. She had grown up in an orthodox Jewish household. When we first met, part of what led me to dive in with her was a quote she shared from the Zohar, the central Kabbalistic text.

"When two people come together in this world, but not out of love, they bring forth souls who have nothing to do with them."

I had no idea if this was true in the case of my parents and me, but the fact that Rebecca might even consider such an idea was a great lure.

Plus, in the '70s, Rebecca had left Jewish orthodoxy and joined the inner circle of Swami Muktananda and his Siddha Yoga movement. Muktananda was the premier Shaktipat guru in the West, with thousands of followers, and lots of teachings for both before and after Shakti awakens. He also, it was later revealed, abused many people in his organization, including underage girls. This tragic story, all too common with charismatic spiritual leaders, leaves betrayed followers to determine for themselves which aspects of the teachings are worth salvaging.

Fortunately, Rebecca had gone through that process many years prior, so when I called her with my quandary she was able to help me in key ways. Muktananda always used to say, Rebecca told me, that "in the end, Kundalini becomes the guru."

I've never been the kind of person who would worship another human being, so fealty to a living guru was out of the question. But this type of inner devotion could perhaps work for me. Rebecca helped me understand that it wasn't based strictly on obedience, and that I would continue to survive it best by emphasizing the "joint" in "joint project."

In describing her time at the Siddha Yoga ashram, Rebecca mentioned that certain people who received Shaktipat from Muktananda awoke with boisterous kriyas, those spontaneous wild movements and sounds that I referenced earlier. Hearing this brought me to tears. I wasn't alone! There was at least one community in the world that had a place, and a context for those like me. Okay, maybe they weren't fending off demons, but at least we had lots in common.

I was so curious how the ashram would handle us. Like the Holotropic Breathwork retreat I wasn't allowed to attend, the core activity of the community was silent meditation. Rebecca explained that near the great meditation hall there was a separate room reserved just for kriya people. There, they could bark like dogs or twirl like dervishes and no one would pay any mind.

Oh, how I longed for that room. And how I loved that it was neither exalted nor vilified—just a safe place for what needed to happen. Until it was done happening, whenever that might be.

Had this still existed at the time Rebecca described it to me, I would've been there in a flash. But Muktananda died in 1982, and his successor brought a very different approach, with no "rubber room."

◆

Journal, April 8, 1996:

> So strange in the midst of it all to find myself at a Passover seder. Lovely people, not spiritual or religious at all, and with no context to hold everything I've been going through. So I keep mum, all the while marveling at how my own context has been forever altered. My experiences are so outlandish as to seem absurd and crackpot to just about everyone, but they are as tangible to me now as the matzoh on my plate.
>
> Going forward I am destined to be here and away, my same self and not. The frame around everything has disintegrated, replaced with a whole new space of possibility. No matter how I choose to relate to it, or interpret it, the shift itself is indelible.
>
> It's like if suddenly I had three arms, or spoke a language I'd never learned, or pulled UFOs from my stomach. There it is, real or not, and somehow it has to be factored in. Even trying to get rid of it, or denying it, is still a way of factoring it in. So I'm in the same old seder, nothing different with the shank bone or my friends, but it's all floating in something bigger and deeper, something numinous, that suffuses it completely. Same old, but brand new. Recognizing this means that I'm brand new, too.
>
> I've crossed the Red Sea. I'm in the desert now. Hopefully not for 40 years.

7

Beloved, who are You? What are You?

Do you leave us with signs and symbols only? Tablets on the mountain? Redeemer on the cross? Cherry blossoms in spring?

Everything is made of You. But You are not those things. Neither can you be isolated nor extracted.

To hold You is to lose You.

Yet You're there. Always. The essence, not the form. And never the same.

Stop! Perk up! I get a taste of You in that perfect pop song (and the awful one). I catch a glimpse of You in that computer crash.

When I let myself dissolve into anything, with all my heart, You reclaim me.

The sound we make, the vibration of our union . . . gives birth to existence itself.

This didn't happen eons ago. It *creates* time. The big bang is happening now. Every now.

But so what?

What difference does that make?

Beloved, You have parted the veil then left me clueless. I see the projector, but still live in Your movie. Why did You choose me? And for what?

Go ahead—keep shaking my branches. Peeling my bark. Digging up my roots and quaking the very earth that sustains them.

But when You're done with this cataclysm, I beseech You:

Let it be for something.

For Your sake.

Make me a tree of Your knowledge.

Etch Your love in these leaves.

Draw the hungry to our shade.

Serve them my succulent fruit.

◆

Implicit in the above prayer was a question beneath all the others I was already asking: How was I supposed to respond to this complete upheaval of the life I'd known till then?

I knew the answer had something to do with surrender. Clearly, it also included sharing my body/mind and inner space, as well as the joint project. But something more elemental than all that still remained unaddressed. It had to do with attention, and how exactly to apply it on a moment-by-moment basis.

When something happens that we're able to perceive directly, it calls our attention. This is true whether it's external, like a cloud crossing the sun; internal, like a muscle twinge; or a thought, like, *It's time to water the plant.* Once we're aware of something, our most basic choice is whether to keep paying attention or not. We make this choice thousands of times a day. Sometimes it's conscious, and other times it's unconscious. Sometimes it's fast and simple, other times it's drawn out and complex.

If we do decide to keep paying attention, new choices present themselves. Should I observe what's happening passively, or interact with it? Should the quality of my attention be neutral, critical, curious, playful, or

caring? How we behold the object of our attention has a lot to do v
impact, both current and eventual, that it has on us.

Perhaps the most important choice of all has to do with proximity. Do
we keep looking from where our attention is first called, do we pull back, or
do we zoom in? What makes this particular choice so delicate and confusing
is that the kind of distance involved is not exactly spatial. Instead, it's more
about our degree of *merger* with what we behold.

In a moment I'll loop this back to my upheaval, but before that, I need
to briefly unpack the idea of merger from a few different angles: practical,
neurological, and spiritual.

The practical angle is where surrender comes in. It's possible to be
attentive to—and even in complete acceptance of—an experience, while at the
same time remaining a safe distance from it. *Yup. Just got fired. Shit happens.*
But it's also possible to lean toward the same experience, even to sink into
it. *Wow. This time, losing my job really hurts. Like a punch in the gut.* Paying
attention to an experience in this way, while fully sunk into it, allows us to
both feel and heal from its impact. If the experience is positive, the same
approach allows us to extract every last drop of joy. Mindful merger, as I'll
call this, is an active, real-time version of full catastrophe living.

The neurological angle echoes this mindful merger within its own
domain. This was best described to me by the noted brain researcher Daniel
Siegel, MD. During a 2012 interview I did with him for my online series,
Teaching What We Need to Learn (http://teachingwhatweneedtolearn.com/
listen), Dr. Siegel explained that the brain has two separate but related circuits. One he calls the "experiencing circuit," and the other he calls the
"awareness circuit." According to Siegel, when these two circuits are functioning in close harmony, we experience the optimal mental state he refers
to as "integration."

It just so happens that this neurological discovery also dovetails in
an uncanny way with the spiritual angle. The Hindu tradition makes this
correspondence the most explicit. In many forms of Hinduism, instead of

two "circuits" there are two great "forces" that make up all of existence. There is Shakti, the energy of that which arises, and Shiva, the consciousness that beholds what arises. It's said that when Shiva and Shakti are in exquisite union, enlightenment dawns. The aim of many Hindu practices is, precisely, a merger of subject and object achieved through rapt attention. (I asked Dr. Siegel in our conversation if he was familiar with this direct parallel between brain science and Hinduism. He wasn't, but it delighted him.)

Inside this practical-neuro-spiritual triangle, things get really interesting. Because it turns out that mindful merging into an experience not only promotes integration and (perhaps) enlightenment, but it also changes the nature of the experience itself. Sometimes this change is subtle, like the deeper revelation that can happen when one mindfully merges with a painting or a song. Sometimes, as was the case with my upheaval, the change can be huge.

Following my conversation with Rebecca, in the last few days before Martin got back, I began to experiment with mindful merging, even though I didn't have that name for it at the time. I found that it was possible to drop into presence, meet the energy as it arose, and hover just above its trajectory. I could hover in this way whether the energy was acting solely as an inner-experience creator, as a doer, or as both.

When I followed this approach, it was always a more-than-wild-enough ride. That's why, over the ensuing years, I couldn't take part in any of the energy-directing practices that were recommended to me, like chi gong. The minute I tried to direct the energy, it would jump the rails and blast its own path. *Do not attempt to harness me!* was the message I felt in my bones. Most of the time, I obeyed.

When I first attempted to take mindful merging further, however, the effect was astonishing. By further I mean letting go of the hover state, relinquishing all separation, and instead staying raptly attentive as the energy and I fell into one another. This entwining thrilled the energy, supercharged it. It became a fuller version of itself and something different altogether. It met my merger with a palpable response that translated into "Yes! Yes! More! More!"

Together, we took off like a rocket. It felt like science fiction made real, and holy. Like warp drive, on repeat, through escalating dimensions of bliss. The quickening vibration of my body soon took me beyond my body. We were ever-expanding, limitless. Sexual but not carnal. Cosmic. To a degree from which I couldn't imagine returning. Yet I did. The propulsion slowed of its own accord, came to an end, and jettisoned me back into the life of an ordinary guy with Chronic Fatigue Syndrome whose wife had recently left him.

As that guy, I shuddered, cowered almost in the reverberations of the voyage. The rubber band of my being, it turned out, had been stretched way too far. It hurt like hell to come back to my body. Hours later I still hadn't found my earthly bearings. I wanted to, and I didn't want to. I fell asleep in that tussle, between worlds, until the phone rang and woke me up.

◆

It was Martin. Thank God. In almost every way, Martin was the spiritual counterpoint to Theresa. It's not that they wouldn't have respected and appreciated one another, or that I wasn't eternally grateful to Theresa. But she was by nature ethereal, perhaps even more in the other world than this one. I knew that now I needed someone who could get me and this whole un-gettable thing in the grittiest possible way. Someone who wasn't Hannah.

What made Martin perfect was also what made him terrifying. I'd known him for almost ten years. We had met at a Los Angeles–based non-profit called Pro Peace, which was planning a march of 5,000 people across the country for nuclear disarmament. I'd been captivated by the vision upon first learning about it, had left my previous job without a second thought, and had talked my way up the organizational ladder in a very short time. The higher I rose, however, the clearer it became that the organization was in complete disarray. The march was about to fall apart completely because almost no one had signed up. As director of communications, I was in way over my head and had little idea what I was doing.

Martin, on the other hand, was an innovative public relations strategist who knew exactly what he was doing. The founder of Pro Peace had hired Martin as a consultant in a rare act of genius. So the first chapter of our relationship was basically me following all of Martin's orders. This segued into a collaboration with a famous ad guru in which we "pre-created" the march as an elaborate public service announcement (PSA). We knew that the finished PSA would rarely air, due to its controversial content, but our hope was that the filming of this mock march would be a national news story. Our hope was that it would attract enough attention, and therefore enough actual marchers, to bring the project back from the brink.

Our method for making this happen included roping in the Brat Pack and other celebrities to march along with a thousand other volunteers. That was my responsibility. I pulled it off with the help of my aforementioned childhood best friend, Mare Winningham, who had appeared in the quintessential Brat Pack film, *St. Elmo's Fire*. With the additional help of Rosanna Arquette, recent star of *Desperately Seeking Susan*, we also, improbably, convinced her costar, Madonna, to participate.

The PSA itself was a great success, and did indeed make the headlines, but it failed to resuscitate Pro Peace. Upon its demise, a small group of die-hard marchers went forth with a drastically scaled-back version, and I wrote an insider's expose for *Mother Jones* magazine.

Through it all, Martin and I grew closer. He mentored me personally as well as professionally. We'd both grown up on the fringes of the L.A. Jewish community. We shared a penchant for progressive activism, irreverent humor, and a love of world music. But that's where the similarities ended. Martin dropped out of mainstream life in his early 20s and spent nearly a decade at a Zen monastery in Northern California. The monastery abided by Zen's harsh approach to self-inquiry. No tolerance, there, for ornate spiritual visions or scary demons. Martin took to it. He soon became one of the highest-ranking monks.

Even in this stark, confrontational environment, however, Martin encountered shadows and disillusionment. The place turned out to be a cult. He stuck with it for as long as possible. Then, mentally battered, he fled. From there, Martin started a group to help other seekers transition out of cults, and of course to heal himself. This put him in the strange position of knowing the "dirt" on virtually every guru out there. He hadn't lost touch with his own spiritual realization, which kept him from full-on cynicism, but he had zero tolerance for, in his words, "New Age ninnies."

I wasn't one of those, for sure, but how *would* he see me? When he left the country, I was your basic meditating Rumi lover. Now I was definitely out there.

I shared everything coolly, like a reporter, even as my legs and head still throbbed. I braced myself for the worst, which I guess would have been dismissal, distrust, and disapproval of what was happening, with some ridicule thrown in for good measure. If kriyas arise in the zendo, or meditation hall as I learned later, you get hit with a stick and told to stop it. They're called *makyo*—illusions caused by sensory distortion.

Martin's actual response, to my great relief, was gentle and kind. He acknowledged and affirmed every detail of my recounting. Then, he shocked me.

"About 4 years ago," he said, "something very similar happened to me."

Wait—Martin, of all people, had been on these same skinny branches? Why hadn't he told me? Martin replied that he tried, at the time, and I brushed him off to the point that he just clammed up.

I took this in with a hot wave of shame. I'd done to him exactly what I was petrified he would do to me. But at the same time I knew it was a likely response to any such tale, including this book, which might seem rife with inflation, confusion, and massive misinterpretation. When presented with something completely outside one's frame of reference, what else can be honestly offered?

The answer, I know now, are words like, "I can't assess this yet. I haven't experienced anything like it myself. Tell me more." It's through curiosity and further engagement that we're able, eventually, to draw less reactive conclusions. Is this mania? Psychosis? Genuine awakening? And if it is genuine awakening, of what? And is it being met in the most helpful fashion?

But Martin didn't need to go through that process with me. In the same wonderful way that I'd stumbled into an underground exorcist, with Theresa, I now had, with Martin, a dear friend who could grasp all my trials instantaneously.

"Listen," he said. "None of this stuff can be put into words. The best we can do is point toward it. But sometimes it's still helpful to learn how it has arisen in other people, and how they and those around them have dealt with it. So I'm going to send you a box of about thirty books. Read them, or just flip through them, if and when the time is right. Plus, you can call me day or night. I'd like to be there for you in the way I wish someone could have been there for me."

This unwavering support was a gift beyond measure. Something settled in me upon receiving it, although the energy itself was nowhere near settling. Martin and I spoke for hours, that night and over the ensuing years, about how best to thread the needle—not too wide-eyed or capitulating, while also not too stoic or hidebound—with each new manifestation of the Kundalini phenomenon.

◆

Because Martin and I did not need to defend or debate our experiences, and because we weren't looking to assign premature meaning, we were able to entertain any and all perspectives about it. From the beginning of our energy brotherhood, we naturally fell into calling that experience Kundalini. It made sense, since the literature of Kundalini, both ancient and recent, was by far more extensive than any other that addressed the same kind of energetic rising. But we were also aware that Kundalini wasn't the only possible lens to look through.

Cultures that practice Voudoun, for example, worship *loa*, which can be translated as "the invisibles," intermediaries between the Supreme Creator and human beings. Each loa rules over its domain, such as agriculture and love, and has its own sacred rhythms, songs, and dances. Of particular note, loa can manifest themselves by temporarily possessing the bodies of their worshippers. When this happens it's considered a privilege, and it's expected that the possessed person will move, speak, and act in ways not at all dissimilar to kriyas.

It seems worthwhile to imagine how my awakening experience would have been perceived within the Voudoun world, and especially how the community's response to and reflection of the phenomenon might have altered the way it evolved over time. There's no way to know, of course, but mindful merging with a mysterious inner force would probably yield different results where spirit possession is considered entirely common.

As for demonic, or evil and unwanted possession, Martin didn't have any of that during his own intense Kundalini years. He and his box of books did inform me, however, that exorcism exists not just in Christianity, but also in Islam, Hinduism, and Judaism. Each tradition has its own sets of demons, as well as methods of expulsion. Tibetan Buddhism, in particular, contains extensive teachings about spirits of all kinds, how to identify them, and how to engage with them for protection and benefit.

The main religious traditions also feature *temporary* raptures of their own, whether derived from speaking in tongues (Pentecostal Christianity), dervish dancing (Islam), chanting (Hinduism), meditation (Buddhism), and all-night study (Judaism). None of these are the same as a force that wakes up and stays, but there's enough similarity to sense that they are activated through similar channels of body and psyche. So, too, with ayahuasca in shamanism and, on the secular front, with psychedelics like LSD and MDMA.

Martin and I also made room for possible physical and medical explanations of our experiences. People undergoing epileptic seizures often experience uncontrollable shuddering, a la Kundalini, as well as mystical visions. Kundalini energy and epilepsy are obviously not the same, but perhaps there's a link, and perhaps one condition can shed light on the other.

Then there's Tourette Syndrome, which causes bursts of movement and speech in otherwise healthy people. Links between epilepsy and Tourette's are already well established. Plus, the speech bursts that come with Tourette's are usually profane, foul, much to the sufferer's chagrin. We have little understanding of why and how a particular neurological event would stimulate such an impulse to be verbally transgressive, but something similar has always been part of my own Kundalini.

Words come out of me from time to time that I don't choose to speak. This can happen both when I'm awake and asleep. It's a kind of audible version of hearing voices. Actually it's always the same voice, mine but not mine, or the appropriation of my capacity to vocalize. While it often says lovely things, like "I love you," or "Lord Jesus Christ have mercy on my soul," it can also blurt, completely out of context, any combination of curse words one can imagine.

All that reminds me of the famous Rumi line, "Who says words with my mouth?"

Who, indeed?

When I shared this vocalizing with Martin, he counseled me not to put too much stock in it, either the exalted words or the nasty ones. Later, I'll offer some examples of how the same voice can take on a kind of trickster quality and come across like a teasing spiritual comedian. I'll also report the way that it spontaneously begins overtoning like Tibetan monks, as well as chanting sacred incantations in distinct but indecipherable languages.

Through it all, over these many years, I've sought to follow Martin's advice and stay rapt to each new arising, while also levelheaded.

Then, buttressing that intention, there's the confounding case of Suzanne Segal. Suzanne told her own story in a book, published in 1996, called *Collision with the Infinite*. From the promotional copy:

> One day over twelve years ago, Suzanne Segal, a young American woman living in Paris, stepped onto a city bus and suddenly and unexpectedly found herself egoless, stripped of any sense of a personal self. Struggling with the terror and confusion produced by that cataclysmic experience, for years she tried to make sense of it, seeking the help of therapist after therapist. Eventually, she turned to spiritual teachers, coming at last to understand that this was the egoless state, the Holy Grail of so many spiritual traditions, that elusive consciousness to which so many aspire.
>
> This book is her story, her own account of what such a terrifying event meant to her when it crashed into her everyday life, and what it means to her now. Her sense of the personal "I" has never returned, and she lives in that heightened spiritual awareness to this day.

Stephen Bodian, the former editor of *Yoga Journal* who wrote the introduction, found her to be "a fearless, joyful being who radiates love and whose spiritual wisdom was equal to that of the masters and sages I most respected."

Suzanne told her story in an unusually approachable, matter-of-fact way. Her style prompted staid, unbiased, and unspiritual *Publishers Weekly* to rave:

> The utility of this book derives from the clarity with which Segal describes the profound spiritual experience of the egoless state and the sense of emptiness that many spiritual traditions seek to produce . . . Segal's account of her own fear while in this state, coupled with her compelling curiosity to understand that fear, can teach others on this path how to cope with the experience. Many have tried to do what Segal does, but none have achieved such clarity in the task. Segal's book is . . . a compelling testament any pilgrim can understand and appreciate.

re's the kicker. Shortly after Suzanne began sharing her experience iritual teacher, she was diagnosed with a massive brain tumor and fell dead within months. Which raises the question: was her "collision" the result of this tumor, or did the collision cause the tumor? And is it equally possible that the tumor was completely coincidental?

Ultimately, such questions are impossible to answer. Yet to both Martin and me, it's essential to ask them. I've applied similar questions to my own extreme experiences almost every day since they began. Did the energy that woke up in me create all the subsequent disturbances, or did the disturbances give rise to the energy? Were the disturbances more about the energy, or about myself? If they were more about me, did they influence the way the energy was able to, or chose to, express itself? Were the disturbances central to the experiences that accompanied them, or merely insignificant by-products? And finally, how might the different possible answers to these questions shift my overall interpretation of everything that transpired?

To reiterate, asking these questions throughout my experience hasn't been about seeking actual answers. Instead, it has helped keep me open, receptive, and ever curious about each new manifestation. It has allowed me to penetrate the mystery of all that happened without prematurely withdrawing into analysis, opinion, or judgment. This approach, to paraphrase Buddhist scholar Stephen Batchelor, has allowed me to find faith in my doubt.

◆

In light of how much about my experience is unknowable, I didn't write this book as any kind of guide to awakening. It's also not meant as a survey regarding all the challenges that spiritual emergers face. That job has been done admirably over the last two decades or so. One exceptional version of it is the newsletter *Shared Transformation*, first published on paper but now available online, at least in part (http://elcollie.com).

Additional information, gathered and presented in a more academic format, comes from the lab of Dr. Willoughby Britton at Brown University. She and her research partners have been intrigued about the unpublicized adverse effects of meditation and related experiences. The current mindfulness craze, though certainly needed, doesn't leave much room for the idea that people are sometimes challenged, if not endangered, by intense inner focus. At the Britton lab, they have gathered hundreds of such accounts, including mine.

So if my story is not meant as a guide or survey, where might it fit in the annals of initiation? Beyond being a balm for the similarly challenged, is there more to glean from its aberrant aspects? It makes sense to address this question now, because upcoming chapters will present events that were even more dismaying to me than the exorcism and deliverance that came before.

What comes next is remarkable in the way that my awakening went from exalted tribulation to prosaic. The extraordinary, over time, became ordinary. Each day continued to lead to new challenges, for sure, but instead of a crisis it was now just everyday life. How that happened, and how I came to accept it, while still questioning all of it, and especially myself, is our final frontier.

I believe that frontier is vital, and that it calls for vigorous investigation, especially of the specific ways it manifests within different people. That's because cases like mine may give us rare peeks behind the scenes into how our reality is constructed. The "veil" parts and becomes porous, revealing elements of—call it what you will—the matrix, skunk-works, karma, or the heaving of an infinite God as it tumbles into mortal form. Through some kind of aberration, whether glitch or grace or both, we get to witness aspects of the way existence manifests.

These skinny branches, I would argue, sway over the boundary between what we can understand and where the very source of our understanding resides. By hanging out here, with a skeptical but open mind, we have the chance to temper the human excesses which put us all, and our earth, at such great peril.

In a way, riotous awakening experiences like mine offer a petri dish for evolutionary possibility. They may offer even more, for all their mess, than those mystical revelations that allow us to see simply that "we're all one." Unitive experiences are gorgeous gifts, no doubt. They allow us to know, with all our hearts, that we are, in the words of the singer-songwriter Sting, "spirits in the material world." But they don't offer much about how that happens, or how it serves us to know it, beyond the resulting amorphous inclination to love more.

What we need now, to survive as a species, is love in action. We need a new, different, very specific kind of love in action, one that takes into account, and draws upon, the anarchic entirety of what it means to be a human spirit.

Raucous awakeners like me, in the current social and historical moment, may be mutations of a sort. In the parlance of epigenetics, something in our makeup and experience may have turned on certain genes, or previously dormant tendencies that allow for illuminating peeks into the spirit-to-matter factory. We are definitely outliers, and maybe even haywires. If so, I suspect, there is ample insight to be mined from our defects.

Or, put another way:

> My fellow citizens of this hallucination
>
> We live in an altered state
>
> We call that state Reality
>
> We believe that state is more real than other states because it can be measured
>
> Because it follows observable and verifiable laws
>
> Understanding those laws allows us to predict and control events
>
> Across nearly infinite time and space
>
> What an amazing opportunity it is to exist in Reality
>
> How worthy of continuing investigation
>
> Our deepening understanding of Reality only makes it more magnificent
>
> But at the edges of our understanding we encounter anomalies

These anomalies confound us

Most of them, sooner or later, surrender to our comprehension

But some just don't

Instead, they beckon, beguile

Reveal Reality in its bubble

Blind to its source

Oblivious that what decreed its laws

Doesn't follow them

Can't be measured at all

Gives birth to every state

Loves all its children equally

Alters them equally

Plays with them equally

Longs to be known directly

Without altering

But can't

Not possible

Which renders the Supreme Being

Supremely alone

Only able to know itself

Through its own creations

And yet, as its creations

We come closest to it through our own longing

What longs to be seen

Glimpses what longs to see

What longs to see

Glimpses what longs to be seen

But only at the edges

Only in disguise

Only for an instant

Altered

Anomalous

Miraculous

8

At this point in my writing of Surviving the Divine, I got sick. Just a bad cold, but it knocked me out for a couple of weeks. During the downtime I got reacquainted with some of the young, tender, helpless parts of me. I curled up, literally and figuratively. I just wanted to feel better, and to be taken care of.

Since I couldn't write, I reread all my journal entries from the first years of awakening. In the process I found an aspect of the experience that I haven't yet represented here. Perhaps if I hadn't fallen ill, it wouldn't have been possible to tease this aspect out from all the simultaneous intensity.

Allow me to give it voice in the way that by now has become familiar.

> *This is all too much.*
>
> *Why doesn't he just make it stop?*
>
> *Or get help to make it stop?*
>
> *It's like he's entranced by the drama.*
>
> *"So amazing!"*
>
> *"So scary!"*
>
> *"So important!"*
>
> *Maybe so.*
>
> *But so what?*
>
> *I don't want any of it.*

I just want my body back.

My life back.

It's mine!

Isn't Chronic Fatigue Syndrome enough of a trial?

I'm not Job.

I'm little.

Sad.

Weak.

Listen to me!

I will not behave.

I will not suck it up.

I quit.

Take me home.

It's not wrong to need comfort.

Comfort me.

Protect me.

Send it away.

Please!

But the energy wasn't going anywhere.

Neither was I.

We were stuck with each other, tantrums and vulnerabilities notwithstanding.

This is the part of the story when the "roommates" within my body are about to stumble their way into becoming lovers. But I already had a lover of sorts, an actual wife in fact, and everything that transpired between the energy and me for yet another year was still haunted by the specter of Hannah. While the energy continued the hard work of demolishing my barriers to Spirit, Hannah worked equally hard, though unintentionally, to burgeon my capacity for pain.

By pain I mean hurt, loss, grief, anger, resentment, confusion, uncertainty, heartbreak, and more. It all came in a form that was so singularly awful, and unbelievable, with each new chapter surpassing the last, that in a perverse way it felt special. For the time being, I was on emotional tenterhooks sharp enough that the ratio of Hannah to Kundalini in my journals ran about 3–1.

I will refrain from including most of that Hannah material, freely acknowledging that the obsessive hand wringing around it is almost impossible for even me to read. And, I do want to get back to the energy as soon as possible. But sharing the most significant events that occurred during my tortured separation from Hannah feels necessary. That's because I have no doubt that each of these two love stories infected each other deeply. Plus, they were equally instrumental in shaping my metamorphosis.

◆

After our ill-fated Amsterdam trip, as recounted earlier, Hannah and I decided not to work toward premature reunion. Theoretically, this meant that we'd each focus on our own lives. She would use the time to heal and grow and strengthen into someone who could really come back and make it stick. There were no guarantees, of course, but that was the hope.

Practically, this meant that my wife was still living with another man, Alex. The two of them had met when performing in a community theater production of Ibsen's *A Doll's House*. Hannah played the lead, Nora, who decides that she must leave her marriage to a stable, loving husband in order to find her true self. While the eerie echo of her casting did not elude me, I still believed we could transcend its seeming verdict.

Alex was ten years younger than Hannah. He was charismatic, dealt drugs for a living, and was perfectly cast in her actual life as the irresistible outlaw. At first, Hannah was confident that they could be just a fling. After all, she had a thriving medical practice, with scores of people who depended on her cutting-edge expertise regarding women's health, cancer, and immune disorders.

But soon, Alex had Hannah blowing off work, taking spontaneous road trips, experimenting with substances, and lying about it all without a second thought. The hold he had over her seemed designed to take her to hell and back, if she could make it back. His touch, as she described it, was more powerful than any drug. At least one part of her saw through all of this, yet she was captive nonetheless.

Only later, when the fire had long burnt out, did Alex admit to Hannah that the whole affair was a grand manipulation on his part. For now it was still a thrilling descent, which meant that Hannah could make no strides toward me without first breaking free of him. I, clearly, couldn't be part of that at all.

Except that it was the elephant in the room, or a whole herd of them really, whenever Hannah and I talked or got together. I couldn't help but monitor how near or far Hannah seemed from freedom. She sensed this acutely, though I didn't bring it up, as a pressure that just made everything harder. Our times together were unavoidably heavy, laden with anxiety and doom. We tried to keep things light by meeting at the batting cages, or for a row in Tomales Bay, but our attempts just came off as forced.

Then there were times when I couldn't stay quiet, when the whole enterprise felt more like stupidity than love. One of those times occurred when Hannah told me, giddy with excitement, that she had gotten a cat. Since we already had two at home, and since I wasn't even a cat person to begin with, Hannah's decision seemed like a slap in the face to any shared future, and especially to me. When I let this be known she deflated, wishing I could just be happy for a little new light in her life. She also saw my disapproval as parental (Torvald to her Nora), and therefore dug in her heels.

There was lots of writing on the wall, by this point, but something in me refused to read it. With everything else I had to deal with, it was easy just to focus elsewhere. But over time, seeing no forward movement, Hannah and I both decided to file for divorce. We recognized that this love story was over, and that any version of us down the road would need to be less of an act two and more of a brand new start.

One rainy fall day we brought all our shared possessions into the living room and divided them up. There was neither rancor nor drama. We cried, and laughed, and cursed the fates that had led us to this moment.

In California, there was a six-month waiting period for a divorce to become final. With just days left in our waiting period, Hannah came to me trembling, head hung low. She needed serious back surgery, and would lose my ample Writers Guild health insurance once the divorce was official. She told me it was totally okay with her if I proceeded with the divorce, but she didn't want to make that decision for me by not even asking.

I decided to not proceed, to allow her to remain covered. But it wasn't that simple. A little investigation revealed that the late date for our change of heart meant that an actual hearing before a judge was required, and that we both needed to be present. We made plans for me to pick her up on the morning of the hearing.

I drove to retrieve Hannah, feeling trapped, conflicted, signing onto another act of an already completed love story. Still, as I saw it, the alternative was worse. So I showed up right on time, sleepy but resolved, and knocked lightly on the door.

No answer. I knocked louder. Still no answer. I waited, with a sinking feeling, and a deadline at the courthouse looming. Eventually I decided to walk around the house and peer through every window. I spied a sprawling Hannah in the master bedroom, fast asleep.

I pounded on the window till it almost broke, finally rousing her. It turns out that for one of the most important mornings of her life, after having asked me for an enormous favor, Hannah had forgotten to set her alarm.

I told her I wasn't sure about the arrangement anymore. I needed to think. I walked around the block, fuming, assuming she'd spent the night wasted with Alex. After storming the block a second time I decided to go through with the plan. No matter the circumstances, I told myself, nothing trumped the need for surgery.

At this point we were seriously late. To make it in time we had to speed, and then sprint through the halls of the courthouse. Under different circumstances we would have relished the rush as one of our comic misadventures. Instead, a grim fog blanketed the whole proceeding.

◆

With still a few more episodes remaining in the Hannah saga, I notice some impatience with myself in my retelling. I worry about getting distracted by it, about milking it for the cringe factor. After all, the first and second divorce filings, and the twists that came with them, happened months after the energy unleashed. So aren't they gratuitous? Don't they just sensationalize the story?

Maybe, but I don't think so. If I edit out the worst of the tale, I'll be shrinking from the principle of radical inclusion that allowed me to write the whole story in the first place. Plus, that principle doesn't just pertain to this book—it's become a guide for my whole life.

Such radical inclusion is not easy to express, and perhaps even harder to swallow. Given those challenges, I'm going to enlist the help of the Old Mystic in the center of my heart.

Letter to a Young Mystic

This path is not for the faint of heart.

Your yes to everything must be unconditional.

Just as you gaze in awe at the majestic redwood, so, too, must you cling to reverence as the hawk on its limb rips the flesh from a mouse.

A live mouse.

If the glinting sun on an ocean wave swells you with ardor, then swell equally, without reservation, at the tsunami that flattens a seaside town.

And pries a howling infant from its mother's frantic grasp.

It's weak, fake, to proclaim the glory of God only in the throes of elation.

Try it in the pits of hell—God made those, too.

Your crushing depression . . .

Your lover's leukemia . . .

Blind fear . . .

The schemer who steals your promotion . . .

The family man who turns his back on a tortured refugee . . .

The gas chambers and the killing fields . . .

The innocent who rots in solitary, hour after hour, on his way to the electric chair . . .

God's handiwork—all of it.

Blink, shy away, and you're no mystic.

Don't get me wrong. Choose any other path and you still have God's blessing.

But if you choose this one, just don't pretend.

Every moment contains its opposite.

The tenderest touch: a gunshot wound.

A toddler's laugh: the carnage of a freeway pile-up.

Thrill: boredom.

Promise: betrayal.

Can you love all of that?

Can you love the God of the Old Testament as much as the New?

What kind of love is that, anyway?

A feeling? An action? A set of principles?

Is it even possible?

Recommendable?

No, it's not.

Walk this path only if you must.

If nothing less will do.

Sing out in glory, rage, shame, absolute befuddlement.

Nothing less will do.

A mystic's prayer is unstinting.

It wails as it worships.

Puts God on trial.

Takes the fall.

As God is my witness, I am God's witness.

All I see is a part of me.

And thee.

And we.

◆

Even my wife. As she tries to take her life.

◆

Full catastrophe living—the mystic's domain—doesn't insulate us from any of life's slings and arrows. Neither does spiritual awakening. Jack Kornfield wrote a book about this called *After the Ecstasy, the Laundry*. It could just as easily could have been called *After the Ecstasy, the Agony*.

But things *can* be different, if and when the agony comes. That certainly was the case for me when Hannah attempted suicide. To illustrate this, I offer the passage I wrote about it in my first book, *Unconditional Bliss*, published in 2000:

> The door to the gym opened and my friend entered. From the look on her face I knew something was terribly wrong.
>
> I stepped out of my weekly basketball game and approached her. In a voice hoarse with emotion, she told me that my wife had just attempted suicide. The paramedics found her without

any time to spare, and she was now teetering on the brink of death, in the intensive care ward of our local hospital.

As I rushed to the hospital, my palms were sweaty, my heart was racing, and my mind was spinning like crazy. Then, something in me began to shift. I noticed my resistance to what was happening. I felt the contraction that had brought it about.

I let out a sigh. I accepted everything. The woman I loved more than anyone in the world might die at any moment. Furthermore, at least some part of her wanted that. This was true whether I could deal with it or not. I expanded into that truth and felt the fundamental bliss of existence surge right back into my being.

By the time I arrived at the hospital, while still intensely concerned, I was at peace with whatever may come. As a result, I became a calm and powerful advocate at a time when my wife needed me most. For both of us, this was the gift of acceptance. And it might have help saved her life.

Just like my aforementioned article for *O, The Oprah Magazine*, this account was true but scant. When I arrived at the hospital and asked to see my wife, the receptionist looked confused and alarmed.

"I'm sorry," she said, "but her husband is already with her in intensive care." It took me a moment to understand her. Then I felt queasy. Then I got mad.

It turned out that Alex was the one who'd found her, overdosed on their couch with a note by her side. He'd given her mouth-to-mouth, called 911, rushed to the hospital behind the ambulance, and lied about his status in order to obtain visiting privileges. Following protocol, the receptionist called Security to sort things out.

While waiting for the officer to arrive, humiliated, I breathed deeply to keep from losing it. I checked for the energy inside me. It was still there. I checked my heart. It was still open. The hospital light, harsh at any time, now cast a surrealistic glow. Was this actually my life? It didn't feel like my life.

The security guard listened to me blankly and checked my ID. His main aim was to avoid an altercation on the premises. After a round of shuttle diplomacy between the waiting room and intensive care, he worked out a staggered visiting schedule for Alex and me, as well as access routes that allowed us to avoid running into each other.

Cleared, I rushed upstairs. Hannah was awake, restrained at the wrists, thrashing from side to side with a feral look in her eyes. Intubated, unable to talk, she struggled in vain to communicate. It took a number of guesses to figure out that she wanted the tube removed. I asked the nurse on duty if that was possible. At first she ignored me, then looked at Hannah with disgust. A suicidal drug abuser, I could tell, didn't merit much regard in her view. She explained to me that Hannah was temporarily delusional from the overdose, the antidote, and the stomach pumping.

I stayed quiet and polite, recognizing that the best way to plead Hannah's case was to come off as an upright citizen. After a few minutes the nurse agreed to remove the tube as long as Hannah remained quiet. The deal didn't turn out to be necessary, though. Once the tube was out, Hannah immediately fell asleep.

As she slept, I watched. I felt shaky with adrenaline, exhausted, still like this wasn't my life. Yet, I kept choosing it. I kept getting drawn back into Hannah's turmoil. Maybe I was just stubborn. Maybe it was like when my parents thought I'd never be able to stick with being a vegetarian at thirteen, so I remained one for years in part just to spite them. Maybe it was like when I came home from Israel instead of immigrating, in part because Mrs. F. swore I wouldn't.

Could I actually walk away at this point? I contemplated the question seriously. I decided that, yes, it was possible. Recognizing that, I concluded that the only way it would serve me to keep helping Hannah was to surrender any attachment to outcome. Whether she lived or died, got clean or kept using, I'd face the results head on, one moment at a time. For better or worse, codependent or not, I still needed to accompany her through this.

There was no pride in this decision. It felt obvious and inevitable. True or not, I told myself I wasn't doing it for her anymore. I was doing it for me. This reorientation opened me up to a new degree of freedom that was quiet yet exhilarating. Not needing a particular ending, surprisingly, suffused every moment of the story with even more poignance.

◆

Once Hannah was stabilized, I used all my pluck and perseverance to get her from a shoddy public facility to a better private one also covered by insurance. Still, it was a psych ward, which added to the haunted tone of the whole episode.

Hannah soon became cogent, and contrite, proclaiming on her own that the choice was to leave Alex once and for all or die. She chose the former, and gave instructions not to let him visit. Together, we set about finding the best possible rehab facility for her. This turned out to be tricky, because she wasn't addicted to a substance or an activity but rather a person, and at the time there wasn't really a program for that nearby.

In the end we settled on a six-week outpatient addiction program paired with a secure, no-visitors halfway house. After all the forms were filled out and the approvals in place, Hannah made the move.

By design, we had little contact over those six weeks. The fewer outside influences for Hannah, including mine, the better off she'd be. The next time I saw her in person was at the outpatient program's family day. Hannah introduced me as her husband, and treated me that way, too. She was gracious, grateful, and grounded. Humbly, she shared the hard truths she'd had to face in the program, both with everyone assembled and also privately with me. I didn't harbor any hopes or illusions that a short stint such as this one would be completely transformational, but it seemed like the best possible beginning.

We made a plan for Hannah to come stay with me at the end of the six weeks. It wasn't clear how long that stay would last, but there was more than enough room in my new apartment and neither of us felt the need to put a time limit or definition on the arrangement.

Before it began, though, Hannah wanted to spend a few days alone in nature. That seemed like a good idea to me, too. I waved with quiet relief as she drove off to Yosemite.

While she was gone I ran errands, worked out, and readied the apartment for her arrival. I also called our mutual friend, Katie, to fill her in on how things were going. Katie sounded very agitated as we spoke. Something wasn't right, but I couldn't tell what. After a few rounds of evasion, Katie came clean.

She and Hannah had spoken. Hannah hadn't gone to Yosemite. She'd gotten in touch with Alex, who had retreated to his home state of Michigan. He'd invited her to join him for a few days. She'd lied to me once more, headed to the airport, and boarded the first possible plane.

It was as if the suicide attempt had never happened. The new resolve that followed, and the recovery that grew out of it, was a wish that just wouldn't take. Like it or not, she wasn't done with Alex, nor the darkness he represented.

I was too wrung out to be mad, or surprised. Plus, I had truly surrendered the outcome. Mostly, therefore, I was resigned. And sad. I could no longer imagine any way for us to reestablish trust, equality, and health. No matter how profound some future healing for Hannah might be, our path back to one another was fully scorched.

There was still another year before I said goodbye to Hannah for good. By then Alex was long gone. So were the drugs and instability, for the most part. Hannah moved to San Diego, and landed a prestigious job as a medical lecturer.

What wasn't long gone were the lies. Not to anyone else, just to me. I caught her in a small but telling one, when nothing was really at stake except her imagined disapproval from me. Just as I had so much trouble letting go of my projection of Hannah as the poster child for innocent victims, she just couldn't shake her own version of me as the reproachful rescuer.

So we turned out to be Torvald and Nora after all. In our case, however, it was both of us who needed to leave.

9

Until now, I've been a bit all over the place in addressing the veracity of this account. First, I said that everything I'm sharing is completely true, but at the same time I advised not to take my word for it and instead just surrender to the story.

Then I wondered if the most far-fetched details of the tale may have appeared true to me because I had gone mad or become psychologically split off. Along the way, when it was all happening, I wrestled myself with how to regard it. I looked through the lens of science, spirit, personal reflection, and common sense. I struggled to find clarity then and I still struggle now, not just with prose but also through poetry and prayer.

So is it true? Yes. I hereby vow that I have not added a single exaggeration or embellishment. But that's only one part of the answer to this question, because each reader is constantly going to revisit it in his or her own way.

Before adding a new slew of confounding elements to the mix, I feel called to take one more brief spin around the subject of credibility. Not just an investigation of mine, but of credibility itself.

◆

"Is that a thing?"

In American slang we ask this question to assess the validity of what's being described.

Chocolate beer? Sleep texting? Mustache mascara?

"That's not a thing."

We use this verdict to refute an urban legend, cultural assumption, or any other type of sketchy claim.

Though overused and out of date, the thing trope persists. I think that's because, with an edge of humor, it swiftly gets to the bottom of, well, things. But, of course, this thing determination isn't always black and white. While some things are definitely a thing, and other things definitely aren't, the majority of things, perhaps, don't turn out exactly as described but do exist in some form, nevertheless. The term "freshman fifteen," to take a random example, refers to the amount of weight that college freshmen put on during their first year away from home. Studies have shown that this is not a thing, yet on average, freshmen do actually put on more weight than the general population over the same period.

All of this, however, pertains mostly to the objective realm, in which something can be pointed to, evaluated, measured, or confirmed externally. When it comes to the subjective realm—"I'm sad," or "You and I were meant to be together"—thing-ness is much trickier to gauge.

Still, we do it all the time. We have to. When a violent person claims to be hearing direct orders from God, we dispute that. We say it's not a thing. Instead, we call it mental illness and treat the condition with drugs and therapy. If those are unsuccessful, we lock the person up.

But what about when a subjective situation is benign? When nothing is at stake? For those times, we tend to rely on intuition, a personal appraisal based on our entire life experience that can't and doesn't need to be verified. Constantly, without focusing on it, we're using our intuition to determine if and how much a topic of our consideration is a thing. Astrology? Feng shui? The Law of Attraction?

In order to explain why I'm addressing this, and how it relates to my love affair with the energy, let me offer a few personal illustrations. I'll begin with cats. As I've mentioned, Hannah brought two homeless cats into my life during our time together in Sonoma County. The first was a gentle male kitten we named Felton, after the mountain town near Santa Cruz and also after a character in one of my screenplays. Though I wasn't easy to win over, Felton soon melted my heart and we became steadfast pals.

The second cat was a tiny, feisty female kitten we named Bundschu after our favorite winery. Soon her name got familiarized to Boonie, and then just Boone. She arrived when Felton was almost a year old. When we let them discover each other for the first time, Felton sized Boone up, paused, and then bopped her ceremoniously on the nose. It seemed to seal their lifelong deal—she was free to run moody circles around him but he would always remain in charge.

During the part of our separation when I was still living in the rambling Sebastopol house, a huge, stray, orange tabby decided to make a home under the deck. Felton and Boone steered clear of this interloper, and for a time he didn't bother them. But then, one day, he figured out our cat door and started coming inside. It took a lot to shoo him out. He acted like he belonged there, or even owned the place. Felton and Boone took great offense, of course, but they also weren't big or brave enough to confront him directly.

Short of capturing and taking the stray to a shelter, I didn't know what to do. And that would have been my last resort, because I didn't want feline murder on my hands and no shelters in the area had a strict kill-free policy. When I was sharing my travail at Carol's chiropractic office, one of the receptionists suggested I consult a pet psychic.

I had no idea that pet psychics were a thing. As soon as possible, though, I set out to find one, sure at the very least it would make for a great story. Since this was the Bay Area, a highly regarded pet psychic was only two degrees of separation away. Within a day I had a phone appointment.

The psychic, I'll call her Peggy, "tuned in" to all three cats and went silent for a while. Then she pronounced her findings. The situation was indeed dire. My cats were miserable, and Felton in particular was thinking of running away. The stray, according to Peggy, was a gangster with me during our past lives in the Roaring Twenties. One of our deals went south, and he believed I owed him. He figured that if I took him in, now, that would make us even.

Peggy said that she explained to the former gangster, through their psychic connection, that this method of seeking restitution was unacceptable. She offered an alternative: I find him a home to live in and we all consider the matter closed. The stray agreed. There was only one problem—all the local pet adoption programs were run by those same shelters that put cats down as a last resort.

Peggy told me about a vet she knew that might help. Sure enough, the vet agreed to offer the stray for adoption through her office as long as I paid for an ad in the local paper. I couldn't place that ad fast enough, and was thrilled when the call came a couple of weeks later that the stray landed a new home. In the process I found my own comedic justice in the fact that the new adoptive parent, who already had one orange tabby named Mango, decided to call my mob associate Pineapple.

Take that, Pineapple!

I wanted to tell this story because it cracks me up. But also because it led me to decide that pet psychics really aren't a thing. That might seem obvious to you, and the whole escapade might come across as ridiculous from the outset. Or, you may have had a positive experience with a pet psychic and think of me as cynically dismissive.

Whether you believe pet psychics are a thing or not, or land somewhere in the middle, or find yourself agnostic about it, rest assured that there are countless other people of great goodwill who land elsewhere on the continuum. It's like that, and will be forever, when it comes to all things supernatural.

But there's another aspect of this story that makes it compelling to me. If I hadn't taken my journey into the iffy domain of gangster cats, I never would have learned about the helpful vet. In other words, a metaphysical lark led straight to a practical solution. And in my experience, things like that happen all the time. They're not quite synchronicities, in the Jungian sense, but close. When I take initiative in one way, my goal often comes to pass in an entirely different way. My intuition tells me that success often works like that. I call it "parallel possibility." And I'm pretty sure it's a thing.

◆

Let's jump ahead about a decade. I'm sitting with two women who have just participated in my workshop. One says to the other, about me, "I think he runs a lot of Archangel Michael energy." The other says, excitedly, "I was thinking the same thing!" Honestly, I have no idea what they're talking about. Is there actually a thing called Archangel Michael energy? Not that I'm aware of. But then, before my demonic possession, I wouldn't have been aware of that, either.

Taking my own counsel, as described in chapter 7, I tell these women, "I can't assess what you're reflecting. I haven't experienced anything like it myself. Tell me more." When they do, it seems like Archangel Michael, to them, represents a positive, protective, purifying quality. Had they said that at first I would have easily understood. So from this encounter I learn something else: sometimes the artifice of description, or even a name itself, precludes the chance for shared perception.

Call the source of all creation God and some people cringe at the religiosity. Call it The Divine and others sniff out blasphemy.

The map isn't the territory, for sure, but now we can also see a further peril: the difference in our maps may keep us from realizing that we're standing on the very same ground.

On the other hand, sometimes we just have to accept that, regardless of any distortion in our maps, we may actually be worlds apart. I learned this when studying the work of John Perkins, a self-described "economic hit man" who transformed his life through shamanism. Perkins became passionate about the art of shapeshifting. He says, quite plainly, that he has seen indigenous people from the Amazon turn themselves into trees, or appear at a specific place in one moment, and a hundred feet away the next.

Reading these passages, I stopped short. Did Perkins mean that such feats appeared to happen in dreamworlds? In ayahuasca-induced hallucinations? In the "imaginal realm"? Or, did he mean that these events occurred in the world of our observable, independently verifiable reality?

It turned out, best as I could tell, that it was the latter. But if it were true that a person could temporarily become a tree, that would mean many people could also witness this simultaneously, even if they didn't believe in shamanism. In fact, the human-to-tree transformation would have to show up on video as well. This, certainly, wasn't what Perkins meant. So while I appreciated the lessons he taught, I came to see that I didn't believe their origin as described. Human-to-tree transformation was indeed a thing, I concluded, but not the thing that Perkins presented.

One last cautionary tale from this arena. The late Candace Pert, an eminent scientist, wrote an influential book called *Molecules of Emotion*. In the book she described how people with Dissociative Identity Disorder (previously known as Multiple Personality Disorder) displayed different health conditions depending on the particular personality present. One personality might have diabetes, for example, while another personality, in the same body, might be in perfect health.

This claim stopped me short as well. If it were true, the phenomenon of different medical profiles would violate the laws of physics. It would therefore require extensive study, and be front-page news. Yet no one was paying much attention to it.

Unable to contain my curiosity, I set out to find the original studies that presented this evidence. It turns out, as far as I could tell, that there were none. The most likely scenario was that unverified anecdotal reports, passed around long enough, had acquired a veneer of authenticity.

In this case otherwise credible experts (Pert and many others) made a false claim about *objective* reality. No need, here, to make allowances for subjective perception or supernatural matters. Different medical profiles for multiple personalities: not a thing. At least not scientifically substantiated.

As I set out now to describe my everyday life in the first years after awakening began, I'm doing my best to keep all this in mind. Accordingly, I'll also do the best I can to share experiences as they occurred in the objective realm. In most cases I'll shy away from interpretations, and subjective impressions that make it easy for us to get separated by our maps. This should simplify things. Either they happened or they didn't. Each of us gets to decide.

◆

To me, of course, the energy was always a thing. This determination wasn't philosophical or analytical—I didn't have the luxury of such remove. Every day presented an onslaught of direct experience, and my most vital job was to hang on. However, it was still imperative for me to keep asking what kind of thing the energy was, not just to stay open and receptive, as described earlier, but also because that conclusion would dictate my approach to it.

If I deemed the energy benign, then I could relax into its ever-evolving manifestation. If I decided it posed some kind of threat or problem, like a mental illness, in full or in part, then it would make sense to try moderating it with medication and therapy. And if I concluded that the energy was divine or spiritual in nature, then it would follow to look for the best possible ways of aligning with and assisting it.

An additional way of approaching the energy was to fully distinguish its source from the side effects, both physical and mental, that it wrought. In this case I would honor its arising as divine but all the complications of that arising as signs of my own wounds, flaws, and karmas. This is the most common orientation passed down through the Kundalini literature, and for the most part what I settled on. But it still left me to my own devices with lots of practical questions.

Should I meditate more or less? Should I go ahead and take medication, or at least supplements to support my body/mind? Should I eat vegan to stay light and supple, or consume lots of meat to keep grounded? Besides continuing to see Theresa, should I follow up the exorcism with other types of energetic purification?

For the most part, in regard to all these practical concerns, I kept experimenting to find whatever worked best. That meant looking for the options that caused me the least physical discomfort, and that allowed me to live my life with as little disruption as possible. I did employ lots of supplements and holistic treatments, but shied away from pharmaceuticals. I wasn't against them on principle, but they just felt like the wrong tool for this particular challenge.

Apart from all that, there remained one more thorny issue: what kind of thing was I? Another way of asking this question was to consider why the whole thing had happened to me. Was it accidental or purposeful? Did it designate me as remarkable somehow? In a good way, a bad way, or both?

Even though I knew these were answerless questions, I recognized that seeing myself as special in any way was a trap to avoid at all costs. And the best way to avoid that trap was to view my relationship to the energy as an *opportunity*. I was an ordinary person in an extraordinary situation. Whatever had brought it about, it was up to me, now, to make the most of it.

Still, one related question nagged at me most of all. Why, out of all the possible options, had my assignation with the energy happened in this particular way? I was well aware that many tales of Kundalini awakening were neater, easier to decipher, and followed more traditional spiritual tracks. Mine, by contrast, was so bizarre and all over the place. Did that have something to do with me? Does the energy's expression, apart from the inevitable kriyas, somehow morph to match its host?

While this question, too, was unanswerable, it intrigued me because many times in my life I had felt like no one really "got" me. I considered myself an involuntary outlier. Things often happened to me in the least conventional way. My Chronic Fatigue Syndrome symptoms, for instance, were out of the ordinary and indecipherable to practitioners of every type. Relaxing breathing practices, to take another physical example, almost always gave me anxiety. And then there was that Vietnamese boat person I sponsored in the late '70s. While his fellow refugees took all the support they could get to start a new life in the United States, he, by contrast, resented every type of assistance I offered.

To this day, I still wonder if the energy skewed so weird with me at least in part because I identified, over-identified, or perhaps even misidentified with the outlier story. This idea seems especially compelling when taking into account the phenomenon of "wakewalking."

wakewalking (noun, new, for my personal lexicon):

Involuntary physical actions performed while one is observing but not interfering; a conscious, dynamic trance, in which the source of volition is unknown and outside of ordinary will.

In one sense, everything that has happened to me since the energy arose could be considered wakewalking. I've already described multiple experiences in which I found myself doing or saying something without consciously intending to or understanding it. But I created the term specifically to highlight a category of activity that began, post-exorcism, when things had been a little quieter and less scary for a while. What distinguishes wakewalking is that these actions seem like they're trying to express something. They're usually insistent, but bluntly imprecise. There's a feeling of meaning present without quite being able to confidently capture it. In response, the insistence grows, like that of a toddler frustrated at not being able yet to master a new movement.

My journals from the time are filled with dozens of wakewalking episodes, many repeated multiple times with subtle differences. Any one of them could have been alarming individually, but, paradoxically, their frequency rendered them less upsetting.

That's not the case, though, with the first episode. It started out innocuous enough, then soon took a completely unexpected turn. I don't actually have a journal entry for this experience, which occurred about three months after the energy first woke up, but I can remember the details as if it happened yesterday. For the sake of immediacy, I'll tell this part of the story through a journal entry that might have been.

I return home from basketball totally spent. Each step up the stairs comes with an ache and a groan. I run the bath super-hot and sprinkle in a heaping scoop of Batherapy. I make sure my homemade contraption is securely in place to allow the water to fill above the safety valve. With more aches and groans, I untie my high-tops, yank them off, and yank off my remaining clothes as well.

I step into the tub gingerly and let my feet and ankles acclimate to the temperature. I do the same for the rest of my body, little by little, until I'm submerged up to my nose. I lie nearly flat, breathing deeply, consciously letting the heat penetrate my pores. I alternate between replaying the game highlights, and letting my mind wander. I almost drift off to sleep.

Gradually I become aware that my body is vibrating. It starts at a low hum, then increases in intensity over a minute or so until taking on a propulsive quality. I allow it to lift me out of the water, stand me up. My sense is that I could stop it but I don't want to. It's mysterious, alluring. Without fear, I let it lead me.

The vibrating energy steps me out of the tub. I'm dripping all over, but there's no reaching for a towel. Instead, in slow, deliberate steps, I walk into the bedroom, around the bed, and continue to the balcony. I open the sliding glass door. I wonder where this is leading. I still feel safe and willing, but with a slight vigilance now as well.

The inner vibration intensifies, as if nearing its destination. One wet footfall after another, I'm led to the balcony's edge. Then, my right leg lifts off the ground. My hip swivels so that the leg can swing all the way out and up. It lands flat against the top of the ledge.

My two hands clasp the balcony ledge as well. My vigilance spikes. Should I let this continue? One part of me longs to let the energy take over completely, as if surrender is part of the mission. Another part of me senses that something is wrong, and that I should intervene at once.

Time seems to suspend as these two responses tangle and compete for supremacy. Thrilled? Scared? Am I one or the other or both?

In these moments of indecision the energy doesn't wait. My hands push down on the top of the ledge, aiming to hoist my left leg next to my right. Before this happens, my mind flashes forward. I see myself on the ledge in a full crouch. I feel an incredible power in the crouch, as if preparing for takeoff.

In an instant I understand everything. This energy wants up and out. It doesn't know the limits of the body it's inhabiting. It doesn't care about that body. It doesn't care about me. All it wants is to fly.

In that same instant I realize that if I continue to surrender, even just a little longer, I'll find myself leaping off the balcony. I'll land arms outstretched on the concrete below. I'll shatter. Maybe die.

At this realization, my survival instinct kicks in. It turns out to be stronger than the longing to surrender. In one reflex my whole body springs away from the ledge. I land in a jangled heap. Breathless, I scurry backward through the sliding glass door. I reach up hurriedly to slam the door shut and lock it. In shock, but back in charge, I grab a towel from the bathroom, head downstairs to the safety of the first floor, and curl into a ball on the carpet.

After the adrenaline rush subsided, I began a reorientation toward the energy that would last for many days. This time, I recognized, there was no demonic attachment directing what had occurred. The ledge experience, scary as it was, never felt dark or malicious. Whatever it was, and wherever it came from, the energy felt misguided. While it seemed to possess the intelligence of the whole universe in its forward thrust, it was also naive, ignorant of both its own impact and of the most basic aspects of incarnation. It seemed neither cognizant of those details nor capable of becoming so.

This meant that I, alone, was responsible for my survival and self-care. My yes now wasn't enough. I also had to learn when and how to say no. It was one thing to understand this conceptually, while not in the throes of a risky episode, and fully another to precisely time and assert that no when suffused by the energy's gravitational pull.

It came to feel like the yes and the no were equally necessary, and that the evolving relationship between them mirrored the dance between my personal body/mind and the energy itself.

When I told Martin about this, he shared his own similar challenges. While his spiritual Disneyland had been less intense than mine, he still found it necessary to bargain with his awakened energy. "You can do anything that you want," he told it. "Just don't kill me."

I deeply appreciated hearing that. It soothed me. Yet, to be honest, my version of the awakened energy was rarely in a negotiating mood. Mostly, as you'll see, it seemed to scoff and bristle at such rational engagement.

Especially when it came to sex.

10

Regarding sex, and the yes/no challenge, I was awash in confusion. What expressions of Kundalini-connected sexuality were desirable, or at least benign? What versions of it were potentially hurtful, and therefore out of bounds?

This confusion arose, in part, because the energy itself was so sexual. The ancient teachings describe it as generative, the primal source through which matter, and even existence, is born. Those same teachings are rife with warnings about what can happen if this drive toward conception isn't kept in check.

In an impure person, we're told, rampant Kundalini can become an amoral and irresistible seducer. It can sow lustful chaos, leaving decimated lovers in its wake.

Was I an impure person? Since my own opening to Kundalini was unintended, rather than through dedication and practice, was the danger, at least in part, about me?

In considering this question, I remembered something my therapist, Rebecca, told me when I had reached out to her at the energy's onset. She said Kundalini wouldn't engage with aspects of my personality that remained in darkness, that were unhealed and therefore unintegrated with the rest of me. So no matter how much transformative light the energy had to offer, I could still pervert it by attempting to leapfrog the basic work of psychological healing.

As shared previously, I had always been very sexual. I explored freely in the erotic realm. Some of those explorations, for sure, were more raw in tone than others. But where was the dividing line between a healthy sex-positive attitude and an unintegrated wound that manifested in a sexual way?

Since I wasn't having sex with anyone else at this time, the exploration of these questions had to do with Kundalini and me alone. And whether I was healed or not, Kundalini proved to be my wildest, most confounding lover. In this realm it didn't want up and out. Instead, it wanted in. But why? Was it teacher, master, trickster, or provocateur?

◆

Once the energy awakened, many of my meditation sessions would often include masturbation. These were wakewalkings in the sense that, as on the balcony, I would let the energy run while being aware I could stop it at any time. But in actuality, I rarely did.

More about that soon. But to better frame the issue, let me jump forward for a moment—about two years after the balcony experience. It was then I went to see a Tibetan healer. He scanned my energy field, chanted, and rang small bells along my spine. Then he pronounced, adamantly, that I should not allow the energy's expression to include any sexual touching. I was wary of this direction, but at his urging I decided to experiment with a firm "no."

I began my next morning meditation with a clear boundary: no hands-on stimulation. In response, a few minutes later, the energy rose and intensified, and the urge to touch became overwhelming. Still, I stuck to my plan. If touching happened, the session would stop.

For a while this test of wills was at a stalemate. But soon, in response, the energy began looking for other avenues to get its way.

Suddenly I found myself flung off the meditation bench on top of some nearby pillows. The energy proceeded to use the pillows like a loophole, creating friction without directly violating my boundary.

In response, I felt a strange combination of anger, surprise, and curiosity. I wondered whether it was time to broaden my no. It turned out that in this particular instance, I couldn't. During later sessions I could, but my veto was always met by the energy's fierce attempt to break free of its restraints.

◆

What I'm about to describe next is probably the hardest part of this story for me to make peace with. To normalize it is out of the question. While I did become accustomed to much of it over time, I'm still clear that this part of the story is bizarre and potentially disturbing. What I'm not clear about, honestly, is how much significance it has for anyone other than me.

And so, I hesitate. I listen to a train of thought that says, "Just tell it how it happened. Let readers come to their own conclusions."

I listen to a contrary train of thought that says, "Of course tell it how it happened, but provide enough context so there's at least some possibility of a soft landing in the reader's mind."

I listen to a soothing, coaxing train of thought that says, "You've already been letting the story breathe. You've already tried to present the outlandish in ways that foster understanding. You've already attempted to approach the ineffable with passion and reverence. Just trust yourself. Keep doing what you're doing."

Okay, then. I'll keep doing what I'm doing. I sense that if readers can make it through this chapter and stay with me, we'll likely remain together till the very end. And if for whatever reason, they decide to jump ship, I need to accept and respect that, too.

◆

I'm reminded, at this point, of Bonnie Greenwell's observation that people experiencing a serious mental break can't tell you at the time what's happening to them clearly. In my case, when overcome by the strange, dark, Shakti-meets-sexuality enactments that follow, I let them overtake me while doing my best to notice everything. Then, in most cases, I rushed to write it all down before the details faded.

Here's a first example from my journal, date unspecified:

Two months have gone by since I've written, and since I was so shaken by the balcony experience. Everything has been peaceful, blissful, even. But suddenly, confusion. I have to get it all out right away. A couple of hours ago I begin to meditate. Uneventful, the usual coursing of energy with spontaneous toning. A phone call comes that I have to take. I get up to answer it and return a few minutes later. As I resume, the energy takes on a sexual charge. It stands me up, moves me over to the dresser. It grabs a yarmulke, studies it, then puts it down. It picks up a small plastic bag filled with lenses from old pairs of glasses. It puts the whole bag in my mouth, seeming to appraise it somehow, then calmly removes it.

Then the energy reaches into the nearby closet and grabs some physio tubing from my chiropractor. At first it tries to create a loop between my legs and neck but that won't quite stay, so instead it just wraps the tube around my neck. The sexual charge increases as the energy enacts, *but doesn't actually go through with*, auto-asphyxiation.

Eventually, there's an orgasm, followed by the usual end-of-session bow. This leaves me shaken, unsettled and scared. I don't know what this is, or what to do about it. It doesn't feel good, or integrated.

Luckily, I have a session scheduled with Theresa. I drive over and fill her in. We decide to do a session of balancing instead of just letting the energy come all the way out. After a while, when I'm a little calmer, she asks me to try engaging with the energy in a way similar to my previous experience with Voice Dialogue. Doing my best, I ask out loud why it's coming through me in such a rough and theatrical way. For a moment it flares back into frustration, confusion at the question, and then the answer comes out loud, in a reverberating version of my own voice: "Because you try too hard."

This hits home, because while it's true that I've been practicing a radical form of surrender, there's still an element of trying to do everything right. Maybe one just can't try to surrender at all—it either happens or doesn't.

After a moment of mulling this over, I want to know more. So I ask the energy what all the sexual stuff is about. It replies: "Sex is good. Don't worry so much." Persisting, I ask why there's simulated choking involved. This brings up a sudden wave of darkness, but words don't come.

Neither Theresa nor I know what to do with this turn of events. While it doesn't seem like I'm in the same kind of danger as before the exorcism, clearly the energy isn't just love and light. But then, what is it? What is it for? Is it still to be trusted? How can I surrender even more, minus the trying, when at least a part of it feels cruel and destructive? Is that even the right thing to do? Am I back on the balcony again, facing some kind of annihilation (although this time it seems less actual and more showy)? Is this really about me, or the energy, or both? Do I need to find a "no" that sticks? Isn't having to look for and enforce such a no another kind of trying? Do I need to bring Christ Consciousness back into this? Why does this all have to be so intense and disturbing? Mostly it makes me feel sad.

It's worth restating that all the sexual enactments I experienced were versions of wakewalking. I was not the chooser of the actions or events that transpired. They happened to me, and through me, but were not engaged in by me, if "me" refers to the sense of a volitional, in-charge self that all of us carry through our lives. There was no "I" considering a possible action and then following through with it. Nor was there a sense of personal impulse. Instead, these episodes were like daytime dreams that unfolded all on their own. The one choice that I did keep making, out of my own volition, was to not stop them.

I did my best to let both the "me" of the dream and the dream's nemesis act out their parts without interference. The setting of these dreams was always comprised of my body, mind, and voice, along with props plucked from the nearby environment that felt, in the moment, supercharged with significance. Only later, after the conclusion of each episode, would I wrestle with whether such significance pertained to my actual life. I wanted desperately to know if this was a spiritual process, led by Kundalini, with a goal in mind, or was it merely a by-product of the energy moving through me. Did I need to heed it, and grow from it, or was the actual growth going to come from setting it all aside?

To make the best possible determination, I made my way through each new scene with ardent attention, while also in a state of suspended animation.

That's definitely how I approached my next session with Theresa, when it took a new and surprising turn:

> First, there is what feels like twenty straight minutes of wracked sobbing and moaning, eyes closed, tears streaming into my ears. Then the energy surges in a sexual, ecstatic direction. It takes over my body in waves of great trembling. I reach out from the massage table and hold Theresa lovingly by the face and back as my legs spread open. Soon I seem to orgasm, but without ejaculating, and it feels like the experience of a woman. Overwhelming in its ecstatic power. Since I'm fully invested in surrendering, there's no way I can regulate this. Thank God Theresa has good boundaries because otherwise, I can tell, the energy would just go ahead and make love to her, too.
>
> Afterward, Theresa and I share our caution and confusion. She hasn't seen anything like this before. She had, however, summoned the Divine Mother before we began. We wonder if this is how she showed up, like an erotic salve upon my grieving.

Theresa also cautions that she couldn't find a sense of me during the sexual time. She kept reaching for the person she knew, whom she was meant to be attending to, but he just wasn't there. I explain that on my side, that sense of myself stayed far in the background yet was always still present. She's relieved to hear this. As we say goodbye I'm mostly just overcome with the glorious aspect of the experience, like ordinary sex times a million, shot through with heart-centered bliss.

Later:

Bliss aside, I'm disturbed enough by all this to call Martin. He's apologetic, at a complete loss for how best to proceed. He puts me in touch with a psychic he respects, Zan. I immediately call and make an appointment.

Over the rest of the day I calm down. I think more about a question from Theresa: "What if this is actually all you, with nothing engaging you from outside? How would you relate to it then?" And I think about Martin's Buddhist reflection that "there's no actual you, anyway, so what does it even mean to say that something is *not* you?"

I also find myself resentful about the way some of this is playing out. I was already embracing Rebecca's instruction to explore any darkness that arises within me, to see an aspect of the journey as ego-purification. So then why is my face being rubbed in all this? Why does the energy have to be so rough and confrontational when I'm willing to see whatever is necessary? If we're truly on the same side, in it together, why do I feel so manhandled?

Eventually I decide that this energy has come up against a compulsive/emotional/sexual knot within me. Whether all the crazy rituals are a sign of the energy being stuck, or actually working through the knot for my benefit, I can't yet tell. But in light of this conclusion, I also decide to not just let it continue happening. If the energy leads in that direction during a session, I'll stop it. If I can't, I'll stop the session entirely.

To be honest, I see how hard this might be for me. Sex is the arena in which I've always given myself full permission. As long as it involves consenting adults, with no dishonesty or deception, anything goes. I've lived this within myself first, and then with others. I don't even know that I'm complete with the exploration. Yet here I am, under new and extraordinary circumstances, deciding that anything *doesn't* go, for now at least, and with specific regard to this overwhelming energetic "affair."

◆

If someone connects to nonphysical realms through means such as Spirit guides or channeling, and if these connections are helpful and free of difficulty, then there's usually not much need to doubt or challenge them. But in cases like mine, rife with uncertainty and confusion, further inquiry can be crucial.

With that in mind, before continuing, I'd like to return to those two questions from above. To begin, what if this was all me, a grotesque splitting and projecting of my own unconscious or unintegrated drives rather than events involving any kind of spiritual intervention at all?

I don't have additional entries that would indicate my view about this question back then, except for the oft-repeated assertion throughout the journals that it didn't feel like that. Beyond feeling, and from my perspective now, after decades of experience with the energy, the question points me toward the nature of the unconscious.

I'm not an expert on the unconscious, but the experiences that make up this book have led me to craft a possible version of how it may be shaped.

My sense is that the unconscious exists in something like concentric circles. The innermost circle contains aspects of the self that are part of an individual's body/mind. Those aspects include autonomic processes, like digestion, as well as needs, wounds, memories, impulses, and emotions that aren't available to the aware self. Psycho-therapeutic modalities, in large part, are about bringing significant unconscious material from this first circle into self-awareness.

The second circle is home to the ancestral unconscious, which contains foundational themes from one's lineage—parents, grandparents, etc. Here we encounter unconscious material that is *inherited*. This material is part of the self, and related to it, but not generated through the self's actual life experience. For those who believe in karma and reincarnation, the second circle would also be where these imprints on one's overall being reside. Varying by tradition, the territory of such vestiges from previous lives might be labeled as the "subtle body," the "causal body," or the "astral body."

The third circle consists of the collective unconscious, which we first visited in chapter 6. Since much of the material in one's collective unconscious is nonlocal, as discussed earlier, its relationship to the self is more diffuse and indirect. The collective unconscious is the soup from which we're all born and in which we all swim throughout our lives. There's only one collective unconscious. It's essence is communal, rather than unique. What is unique, though, and unmappable, is the way the collective unconscious penetrates and interacts with the first and second circles within any specific individual.

The final circle of the unconscious encompasses elemental energies that exist prior to and apart from history and culture. These energies may remain dormant, like Kundalini, or be universally active, like whatever impacts the cosmos may have on the way human personalities are formed and express. These are the impacts, of course, which are charted and studied in the various branches of astrology. This circle can also function as a kind of border crossing for divine energies. After arising from the oneness that is both everywhere simultaneously and also outside all space and time, divine energies distill here into forms that can then enter our lives in perceivable, yet enduringly ineffable, ways.

From here, divine energies can move inward and permeate the collective unconscious. This is why certain symbols possess such powerful meaning and resonance. Whether religious or otherwise, we experience them as mysterious, numinous. They offer a mesmerizing taste of what's beyond our ordinary perception.

When those same energies cross all the way into the first circle of the unconscious, such as with activated Kundalini, they can't be fully contained and therefore partially burst into the individual's conscious domain. This creates a rare and precious divine-human interface. In the case of Kundalini it may be rough, difficult to navigate. But it also may arise as moments of sheer rapture, in which we come to know our true nature, beyond form, beyond distinctions of what is conscious and unconscious, as boundless love.

All of that, of course, is just one person's conjecture. So how does it relate to the question at hand? I think the main way is that it allows us to refine the question. We can now ask: Which realms of the unconscious were involved in my strange, sexually charged experiences? Is there any reliable way to tell? And if no one else is involved, and no actual harm takes place, does it matter?

If somehow it were determined that only the innermost realm of the unconscious was involved in my experience, then my perception that it was happening *to* me would have been inaccurate. The truth would have been that my body/mind was producing the illusion of an outside force while actually acting upon itself.

If somehow it were determined that the second circle was involved in my experience, then it might follow that an unresolved trauma along my ancestral line, or a karmic knot from a previous incarnation, had somehow broken through to my conscious awareness. In addition, anything deriving from the third and fourth circles of the unconscious would have had to hop the fence in a similar way in order to manifest so vividly as actual, conscious experience.

As mentioned previously, when these events originally occurred I usually defaulted to a first-circle frame of reference. Whether the energy itself was from within or beyond me, what it stirred up always offered opportunities for personal healing and wholeness. In other words, I chose to make it mostly about myself. That seemed the safest and sanest way through.

Yet the entire trajectory of the experience over all the intervening years led in the exact opposite direction. That direction kept dissolving the boundaries between my conscious and unconscious. It also kept dissolving the boundaries between realms within the unconscious. Everywhere I looked I saw less and less separation between myself and what I experienced, and between the possible sources of that experience. As the saying goes, referenced earlier in poetic form, "All I see is a part of me."

Later, I'll describe how I came to adopt that perspective in a more intentional way. In relation to these aberrant sexual experiences, however, what's relevant is that as long as I didn't get too freaked out by them, and continued to do my inner work, they fit with this overall trajectory. They seemed more like tools to wrench me open rather than symptoms of pathology. That was true even when they left me raw, confused, and temporarily terrified. And since my trajectory aimed more and more clearly toward expansion and inclusiveness, toward an identity that encompassed my personality but that also exceeded it, where these phenomena derived from came to matter much less.

Which leads to the second question, the one Martin asked, about what it means to say that something is "not you" when there isn't even an actual you in the first place. Martin's question came from the Buddhist view that the sense of a separate self has always been an illusion, albeit a necessary one to get through life. This view is also quickly gaining credence at the cutting edge of neuroscience research, as referenced earlier in connection with Michael Gazzaniga. In my current conception, the only time that determining something as "not me" would be meaningful is if I'm in some kind of supernatural danger.

For example, if Theresa and I had viewed my demonic possession solely as a personal, psychological crisis, I believe it would have had dire consequences. Perhaps I would have had a complete psychotic break, or disappeared into a fog of drugs. It helps to recognize that even if the demon was ultimately an aspect of myself in the sense that "All I see is a part of me," I still wasn't ready to know it that way. Working with it as "other" allowed me to defang its form, to shift it out of malignancy.

Today, considering the sexual aspects of my journey with the energy, it can be tempting at times to otherize it. That's especially true because it's embarrassing. It can be equally tempting to make it *all* about my own stuff. Doing so would help with the embarrassment, since it would portray me as being psychologically humble and responsible.

But since none of the events involving sexual material ever led me into any real peril back then, and still don't, I'm gratefully free of the need for any black-and-white divide. What feels the most true is that all this erotic theater was primarily about me, but that it also, from time to time, tapped into all circles of the unconscious. It seems likely that when the action most moved me, or spooked me, the scene at hand was functioning on multiple levels.

◆

The following day:

> With my new resolve, I enter the surrendered space gingerly. It begins with some charged breathing. Then, spontaneous chanting. I listen with a mixture of curiosity and vigilance as my mouth forms the words, "kadosh, kadosh, kadosh" (the Hebrew word for "holy"). The chant is rhythmic, soft, and soon morphs into a chant of "Jesus is my Lord," and then after that, "Jesus is my heart."
>
> As the chanting continues, the devotional quality shifts into a more instructive, meditative mode. This passage begins with the phrase, "Now is the time." Eventually it condenses into just, "Now. Now. Now. Now."
>
> All the chanting lasts about a half hour. When it comes to an end I feel blissful, tranquil, and it's in that state that the energy walks me over to the mirror. I look straight into my own eyes as

the words come through. "I love you. You are so sweet." Chants to this same effect continue for another ten minutes or so. It's like a balm for my whole being. In the same spirit comes a masturbation. It is totally in bounds, without anything that I had resolved to stop. I feel a great sense of relief, and renewed safety. The pleasure that comes with it is far in the background, almost incidental.

But not so fast. From later that afternoon:

I'm enjoying time outside in the garden. I'm transplanting and pruning, and making sure to do lots of stretches in between to protect my back and stay present and grounded. I come inside for a snack and suddenly the energy is all over me. This isn't surrendered space, and I haven't even agreed to use this time for connection with the energy, but it comes with a voltage almost as intense as the very first bursts. Because of this intensity and urgency, I decide to let it run and see what happens . . . within the new limits.

For a while the energy pours through me in an unadorned way, causing forceful tremors through my head, neck, and limbs. Then the energy pulls me all the way to the ground. It glues me to the spot while vibrating intensely at the same time. It's a brand new kind of wake-*stopping*, a conscious and pulsing paralysis. I'm taken by surprise, but also somehow more curious than worried. After about five minutes of being pinned there on the floor, little movements begin. Then I get up, collapse again, and the whole thing repeats.

Postscript: I tremble for a while after completing the above account, then fall asleep. Upon waking, I head to the bathroom to pee, and the collapsing experience happens two more times. In the middle of it, I consciously assess the situation. I decide that I'm okay, that eventually I can find a way to understand all of this, to work with it, but then I wonder if I've succumbed to a false sense of security.

The next day:

> The energy begins our designated time together with a long child's pose, followed by a headstand. Then it takes me through two collapses like the ones from yesterday. During those times the energy moves through me in gentle rivulets. I chant the supplication song from *Godspell*, "Oh God, I'm dying. Oh God, I'm dying."
>
> Then I'm raised up and walked around the house in a state of curiosity and suspense. The energy builds for whatever is about to happen next. At my desk I fumble for pen and paper, and then quickly, boldly, scrawl out the words, "YOU ARE GOOD."
>
> Immediately I remember how recently the energy had gone so quickly from light to dark. I wonder if anything at all is still trustable between us. As if reading my mind, the energy responds directly to this question using a quiet, confident version of my own voice.
>
> "Yes, you are good. This isn't a trick. I'm sorry about before, with the choking. It was meant to be revealing. We needed you to know that there is hatred in you, and that it is dangerous. Now that you've agreed to work on that, everything is fine. We won't put you through that anymore. If anything like that ever comes up in our time together with you, we promise it won't be us."
>
> The chanting from *Godspell* resumes, continuing onto, "Oh God, I'm dead," and then, "Prepare ye the way of the Lord." When the chant fades, the same gentle voice returns. It offers snippets of reassurance. "It'll be okay." "Thank you." "Be patient." "You'll understand everything in time."
>
> Then, the bow.
>
> In the aftermath of this communion I realize that for the first time the energy spoke about itself as "we." I also recognize how rare it was for the entire experience to include nothing sexual.

As I remained on the bed, some sexual energy did return. But now it was out of surrendered space, and therefore not Kundalini directed. I decided to experiment with the session's teaching. I met the sexual energy with a wide open heart. I let the sex and the heart blend together. Then I moved from the heart toward an earthier, edgier expression of sexual energy. I watched to see if it still felt right. It did. I explored whether it was possible to experience that edge without any darkness whatsoever. It was. I felt aggression, to be sure, but somehow it remained as wholesome as it was hot.

All of this filled me with relief, and joy. A sense of purpose had returned to the entire wild journey. I had a sudden urge to call Hannah, to tell her I loved her and that everything would be alright. Before I could, though, a wave of fatigue overtook me and I fell fast asleep.

◆

Over the next week, and for a couple of months in total, it became ordinary for the otherworldly presence to speak to me, conversationally, through my own voice. Often it remained plural, as in, "We're back. It's so nice to have a body." Other times it just offered guidance or perspective, without the plural form.

One day it had me chanting the Hebrew prayer-word "kadosh" over and over, after which it suggested that looking up the translation would help me. The prayer contains a name for God that roughly means, "lord of the armies of heaven." I wasn't sure, and the voice didn't offer confirmation, but I got the sense it was telling me that they were indeed a kind of divine committee.

This committee became increasingly interested in my physical existence and the choices I made within it. Often, while in surrendered space, it would change the clothes I wore or create a soundtrack to the experience by selecting and playing songs from my CDs.

Soon this sense of the divine committee became more direct and overt. The voice said, "We are with you always. We are your guardian angels. We're sorry about all the problems you're having with digestion and mental confusion. This is going to take a little longer than we anticipated. If you ever need us, just chant 'om srivat salaya.'"

Except for the "om," I had no idea what this phrase meant, or even if it was actual Sanskrit. So of course I looked that up, too. I didn't know where the word breaks actually were, so I searched the syllables in different ways. I discovered that "srivatsa" is the coil on Vishnu's breast, circling a pearl-like ball at the heart. "Laya" is absorption of the mind. These bread crumbs were exciting to discover, even if I wasn't sure that I had it all right, or what the phrase was meant to teach me. From that point on, though, it became one of the common chants that would arise in surrendered space, and it always filled me with soft reverence.

It was around this time I had the first inclination that all the sex and reverence might in part be a kind of preparation, that it actually could be *for* something and that it might alter the course of my life. Nothing was straight-forward, yet the overall thrust of the experience suggested events to come.

For instance, in one encounter I was led three times back to the book-shelf. The first time I retrieved the *Jewish Daily Prayer* book. I landed on the central prayer of Judaism, the Sh'ma. "Hear O Israel the Lord is our God, the Lord is One." I sang it out three times, as if before a congregation.

Then I went back for the New Testament. I flipped through to the Sermon on the Mount, and read that out loud, too, again as if sharing before an assembly: "Blessed are the meek . . . Blessed are the merciful . . . Blessed are the peacemakers . . ."

The third and final trip to the bookshelf was very different. I grabbed *Pirkei Avot*, a seminal Jewish text which translated as "Ethics of the Fathers." I quickly found my way to a section that, in essence, was about searching for a guru. The energy hovered for many minutes over this passage, as if considering the whole guru/disciple relationship, and how it applied to us.

◆

Let's step away from the blow-by-blow account for a moment and address that question: How *did* the guru/disciple relationship apply to us? Earlier, I mentioned that the spiritual teacher Muktananda was known to say that ultimately Kundalini becomes the guru. I noted, at the time, that while a flesh-and-blood guru would never suit me, perhaps I was better built for such a relationship with an inner kind of teacher. But was that really true? Had I ever bowed fully to the energy in the way required of a disciple?

In case it's not already clear, the answer was an emphatic no. At the same time that I let everything happen, I constantly kept wrestling with it. I allowed and questioned, allowed and questioned, without ever fully trusting. I deemed it necessary to hold my own in the joint project, and also in the yes/no challenge.

Maybe that was the very best path, and just how it all needed to unfold. Yet might it also have prevented me from greater realization? Did it sell the energy short in some essential ways?

Here and now, I'll attempt a more fervent bow, allowing the energy to address these issues in its own words . . . or at least with the best imagined version I can conjure.

Your theories are all so well developed.

Your questions are all so nuanced.

Oh, but if you only knew.

I'm not your problem to solve.

Your puzzle to piece together.

Your interlocutor.

And for God's sake I don't negotiate.

Stop negotiating!

Start trusting!

That demon from before—he works for me.

That bridge you almost tried to drive off—I never would have let that happen.

Theresa—she's *my* angel.

This is all ordained, my beautiful, blind man.

Including your free will.

But you can't grasp that.

You're not supposed to grasp it.

That time on the balcony—the urge to leap, your last second abort—some of my choicest choreography.

How many times do I have to say it?

You try too hard!

Stop trying!

Start trusting!

Or don't.

Because that's ordained, too.

The physio tubing—it was just a strand of Indra's net.

The orgies with spectral beings that you're about to scandalize us with next—they actually happen all the time, on the down low.

It's happening to you right now. And to your reader, too.

Standard operating procedure, in the spirit-to-matter factory.

It would all be so shocking if it weren't so ordinary.

The only difference in your case is I let you sneak a peek.

I tell you this because I love you.

Believe in you.

Hold none of your apostasies against you.

They're annoying as hell, but you just can't help it.

I get that.

I know how hard it is just to be a person.

Held together with nothing more than paper clips and sticky notes.

How do you even do it?

It's a miracle you don't just fall apart constantly, descend into the disorder and chaos that hunts you down every day.

It's always right there. A sniff away. If only you could smell it like I can.

Plus, these Kundalini stories of yours, of ours, are nothing compared to the random human secrets that scroll endlessly through my feeds.

Not even including dreams, those warehouses of ghoulish transgression.

But my one and only soft spot is for you, babe.

You're *my* ghoul.

We were assigned to one another.

If it turns out that you ever can come to kneel before me, to kiss my ring with the pure devotion and obedience that is the mark of true liberation . . .

Oh what a love we'd have!

So much more than this—this whining and grinding and second guessing.

Guess what, my beautiful, blind man?

If you could find a way to fall away . . .

To let go of everything but your body and your breath . . .

Then . . . then . . .

O, disciple . . .

Then you'd finally meet my own master.

Our work here would be done.

We could finally come.

Undone.

As One.

◆

Whether or not it had anything to do with my degree of devotion, the chaos that consumed me wasn't yet ready to distill into something clearer or more direct. The messy mix of sex and spirit, holy and unholy, physical and non-physical remained as confounding as ever. This applied especially to the orgies with spectral beings that my would-be inner guru made mention of just above.

While on a vigorous bike ride through the rolling hills near my house, with nothing but grass and sheep for miles around, my voice erupted in a sexual frenzy. It was the sound of a woman moaning, approaching orgasm. Its energy was purely feminine. The attention I paid to it, while still riding at full speed, was a neutrally observing masculine. As intense as it was, there was no hint of darkness in the entire experience.

The woman eventually had not just one but three orgasms. She whispered to me intensely the whole time as if I was her lover. When it was over, the energy spoke to me in its sweetest voice. It told me that the woman I just hosted was "them." It explained that when I have a sexual episode and invite them in, which is required for their participation, it's amazing. What they hadn't explained before, I was now told, is that they need it, hunger for it, more like a human than an angel. They're so grateful to me for this opportunity, to care for me, watch over me, and especially to make love from inside my body.

This bike ride body-sharing filled me with new questions and doubts. The voice that spoke to me about it felt kind, for sure, but there was also an edge to the experience that gave me pause. I wasn't sure it could, or should, be trusted.

Luckily, weeks before, I had scheduled an appointment with Zan, the psychic and guide to the unseen realms that Martin had highly recommended. The appointment came just days after the bike ride, so it was fresh in my mind and at the top of the list of things to cover.

Zan offered two amazing gifts in her consultation. The first was that she was completely nonchalant about everything I explained. This allowed me to relax, to occupy the world I was being challenged to inhabit without excess fear or tension. It was still an extraordinary new normal, and I still needed to be careful, but having Zan on my team along with Theresa provided a warm, gentle affirmation of my basic approach.

The second gift from Zan was an edict that guided me faithfully from the moment the words crossed her lips. She said, "If it opens your heart, go with it. If not, send it away." Simple, practical. Everything I needed. Zan further explained that I could vet any voice, trance, or entity by asking directly if it was there for my highest good. The way it all worked, she told me, was that this question demanded and would always receive a straight answer. If the answer was no, it was always in my power to banish the threat. Ever since, in my own experience, I have found this to be true.

The rest of what Zan shared was standard-issue future prediction, none of which turned out to be accurate. But I wasn't really in it for that, and my gratitude for her never wavered.

In the weeks following the session with Zan, I could feel with renewed sensitivity when my heart was opening or closing. I used this awareness to turn toward or away from what came through the energy's portal. I also confronted some sketchy-seeming voices exactly as Zan instructed, at which point they went completely silent. It became more and more clear, through these episodes, how keenly I must balance guarding and yielding.

At one point I decided to abstain from all sexual activity for a week. That decision reinforced my confidence as a guard. And when it did feel right to yield, the experiences that followed took on new, ecstatic dimensions. None of it felt personal. It was happening in and through my body, but it didn't really involve me. Trying to capture this, I wrote: "When I get out of the way, it definitely opens my heart. It feels like the divine embracing the divine in a manner that is clearly practiced and well understood to the energies participating."

Not that *I* understood. I didn't. Part of yielding, I gradually came to see, meant giving up my need to understand.

◆

While the sexual storms of my Kundalini experience remain a fundamental mystery to me, I'm still drawn to meaningful interpretations by wise guides. One of those guides is the spiritual philosopher Ken Wilber, who builds upon a Freudian view to maintain that all of us, as infants, live in a "blissful, erotic unity with nature." Wilber says that as infants grow and develop, this state becomes narrowed and knotted in the genitals, and therefore only available through sexual pleasure. He posits that the aim of Kundalini yoga is to help us reconnect with transcendent bliss, to break it out of its genital prison and allow it to restore our ecstatic union with everything.

It makes sense to me that this would also be the aim of spontaneous Kundalini awakening, and that since the original imprisonment of this force is what births and shapes the ego, reversing the process would always proceed in a way unique to each individual.

From that perspective, my own confusing and chaotic journey would therefore be just one out of an infinite array. At the same time, though, since no one gets out of ego jail without going through the genitals, every escape has to somehow be sexy.

Along the way, the blend of personal and cosmic drives must exist in a turbulent, turned-on netherworld. Each landmark, each station of the sexual cross, so to speak, possesses its own unknowable ratio of the sacred and the profane, as well as the personal, transpersonal, archetypal, and universal.

Talk about a hot mess!

◆

The human brain possesses an incessant drive to find and solve problems. My own brain is no different. Despite all my steps toward surrender, the uneasy relationship between the energy and my psyche practically begged for intervention. Beyond the two fundamental questions—1) Is this all okay? and, 2) How do I survive it?—I found myself constantly looking to tweak my approach, to somehow intervene.

This natural tendency to intervene was heightened by the refrain of almost every healer and guide I consulted along the way. The ultimate goal, they advised me, was integration. *Integration.* I heard the term so frequently that it became a spiritual buzzword. My job, therefore, was to hasten the integration of the energy into my organism so that the two would become an indistinguishable whole.

Yet every time I sought to tame and integrate the energy, it only reasserted its autonomy. This was true in all realms, not just the sexual. I tried a chi gong class, as mentioned previously, to help direct the energy in a grounded, time-honored fashion. But with the very first instruction, the energy spiked in rebellion. While the rest of the students easily followed the simple movements, I found myself in a near-seizure, flung about like a rag doll. The experiment was such a failure, and so distracting, that I quickly bolted out of the studio.

In my case, I soon came to realize, striving toward integration was futile. But my problem-solving mind couldn't help looking for another guiding principle. How was I supposed to fix this? What should I *do*?

My saving grace was the late, renowned philosopher of yoga, Georg Feuerstein. Somehow I managed to track him down, to get him on the phone for a few minutes. Georg told me that after all his years of observing the phenomenon of Kundalini awakening, he had come to one conclusion: the energy was self-directed. Any attempt to alter its course would only slow things down and make it all worse.

This conclusion rang deeply true. From that point on I returned to it like good medicine whenever my situation seemed excruciating or maddening. Georg's perspective provided peace as well as patience. It brought me as close to discipleship with the energy as I was ever able to come. It reined in my internal fixer, and allowed me to leave well enough alone.

11

This thing we have

It's like I'm dating a seraph

But in masks and costumes

The way aliens in movies present themselves first in human form

So we can actually relate

But not really dating because we live together

Are we truly lovers, though?

Do you actually care about me?

If so, why do You wrack my body with so many ailments?

Do I need You to care about me?

Or is there something about the impersonal . . .

Think *Last Tango in Paris* . . . that speaks to my . . .

what do they call it now? . . . "Attachment style?"

For as long as we've been sharing this body now, at least You could pay rent!

But no. As Mom always used to say: "Life isn't fair. Get used to it!"

I think I might be getting used to it.

And to You, too.

So . . . Should we make this public?

Are You ready to meet my friends?

In human form so they can relate?

I think I'm almost ready.

As long as you'll behave.

Can you behave?

◆

About a year after my Kundalini awakening began, a fundamental shift occurred in how I related to it. Prior to the shift, understandably, my whole focus was on finding the best possible responses to all these outlandish, mystifying experiences that kept confronting me. But then, gradually, I came to accept that this was my life now. Whether I wanted it or not, my daily existence had become a blend of "chop wood, carry water" and *Mr. Toad's Wild Ride*. No longer was I challenging that cacophonous blend, even as it continued to challenge me.

Instead, my primary inquiry shifted to the person I was gradually becoming. Who was he? How had all this shaped him? Forged in this extraordinary, inexplicable fire, what would he choose to do with his life?

By far the most significant change was that my heart had been blown wide open. At the center of my being was the priceless gift of transcendental love.

I don't mean to suggest that I always felt and acted lovingly. I did and still do get triggered like everyone else. But in a distinction of Ken Wilber's that spoke to me in a new way, my heart opening had moved from a "state" to a "stage." This meant that whenever I consciously brought my awareness to my heart center, that transcendental love was always right there to meet me.

That stage of love that took root in me led to all kinds of new experiences. One example was the difference in bridges. Just months before, I had driven over the Richmond Bridge battling demons. Now, listening to Mike Scott's "She Is So Beautiful," I drove across the Golden Gate Bridge with tears of unimaginable joy streaming down my face.

Another example is that I went from someone who always loved to dance to one who often was "danced" by this radiant love. Literally. During my Friday night visits to "Barefoot Boogie" in Berkeley, I would begin moving to the music in the usual fashion. But then the energy would surge forward from my heart and take over.

Rather than wakewalking, I would begin wakedancing. My movements would become entranced, pulsing, ritualistic. I would face the giant speakers like a wild shaman or a God-drunk dervish. The love in my heart would intensify, expand, pour myself through the world and the world through me until there was nothing else but love making love to love. I never knew when this wakedancing would begin, or end, but it would happen almost every Friday night and leave me in a welcome fever of gratitude and awe.

On a day-to-day level, my basic personality also changed. Before, my intellectual hunger had rendered me a bit of a know-it-all. Now I was still as curious as ever, but much of my arrogance had softened. I knew for sure that I didn't know anything, and that I truly loved everything.

This part of the change was best exemplified through my experience with Thomas and Joanne. They were partners and counselors that Hannah had introduced to me a few years earlier. As newlyweds, Hannah and I had booked a personal retreat with Thomas and Joanne at their ranch in Colorado.

While I got an incredible amount out of the experience, I wrestled mightily with both of them the whole way. Their orientation was more New Age than mine, and I couldn't help objecting and bogging down at each of their questionable or fuzzy-seeming assertions. It was exhausting for everyone, and it never occurred to me that we didn't always need to debate, or agree, or that I could simply note some of my objections silently and proceed without friction.

Following my separation from Hannah, and my entry into the heart stage, I asked Thomas and Joanne if I could come see them again for a solo exploration. At first they almost denied my request, seeking to avoid another round of my peevish grilling. Once we were all together, they marveled at the ease of our connection. "Whatever you're doing," Joanne told me, "keep it up. It's like you're a different person."

The heart stage also became palpable as a quality that expressed without choice or effort. It was just there. I understood this best a few years later, when I was invited to address a gathering of healers. After my talk, I asked one of the organizers how it went, and if I did a good job covering my topics. The organizer told me that while the content was fine, I could have been reciting the phone book. "What really mattered," she said, "was the feeling."

A sweet, unanticipated outgrowth of that feeling was that couples began asking me to officiate their weddings. I had never done anything like that before, but suddenly it seemed totally natural. One of those weddings took place in the hidden Bay Area treasure of Bolinas. The bride and groom were both from prominent families in the Northeast. They asked me to draw upon Jewish traditions in crafting the ceremony, but to keep it mostly spiritual rather than religious. They also really wanted a mention in the *New York Times*.

The fact-checker at the *Times*, unfortunately, couldn't understand that while the ceremony would be Jewish themed, I was not an actual rabbi. Before agreeing to print the wedding announcement, he spoke with me repeatedly, and sometimes heatedly, about the most minute turns of phrase in his proposed copy. I eventually convinced him that we were all legit, and worthy of publication. Along the way I noted wryly that he was a lot like the first retreat me who had shown up to do battle with Thomas and Joanne. The role of stickler, at this point, I happily handed over.

In addition to becoming much softer, I now also lived in two worlds. One world was natural, the other supernatural. But the supernatural world had become just as real to me, just as lived in, as the earthly realm. I could dialogue with the staff at Rocket Science in one moment, then commune with nonphysical entities the next. I could pay my bills while in a spontaneous chant. I could fold laundry while thrust sporadically into headstands.

I could plant a seedling in my backyard garden, fall onto the muddy ground in a twenty-minute embrace, then calmly, dispassionately continue planting.

While shifting, or rather *being shifted* so fluidly between the two worlds, I began to notice how the wildness that ran rampant in me was also hiding everywhere in plain sight. When it's socially sanctioned, and built into pop culture, what otherwise would seem off-putting and alien becomes mainstream, celebrated. Think of giant sports stadiums around the world, filled with deliriously roaring fans. Envision throngs in dark clubs, swaying as one to the relentless beat of EDM (electronic dance music). While it's easy to view the shamanic rituals of indigenous people as primitive or exotic, it's even easier to miss the way our own civilization is invaded by similar elemental energies. Plus, we're constantly intoxicated in one way or another, be it by alcohol, drugs, consumerism, or war.

Even those who tend toward more sober pursuits, who tout the virtues of all things rational, are still often powerfully drawn to the supernatural. They want to be scared by it, as with horror films. *The Exorcist* and its ilk make millions of dollars from moviegoers who would scoff at my actual demonic possession.

Those same skeptical people seek *comfort* from the supernatural as well. I remember vividly watching the film *Michael* on Christmas Day in 1996. All around me in the theater people were charmed at the archangel played by John Travolta. I could tell that the filmmaker, the late Nora Ephron, saw him as a fanciful contrivance. But watching the portrayal onscreen I was moved to tears. To me, in a way, it was a true story.

Along the same lines, let's not forget how magical realism speaks to the truth of our lives in a manner that plain old realism rarely can. And, if there's still any doubt, I submit to you the extraordinary worldwide phenomenon that is Harry Potter.

◆

My supernatural truth didn't just intertwine statically with the natural world, either. It was constantly evolving, propelling me further and further into its depths. The most significant example of this occurred one day when I found myself wakewalking to the bathroom and staring into the mirror. As my eyes locked in on their reflection, slowly my field of vision began to disappear. It was eclipsed by a radiant blue, somewhere between cobalt and midnight, seemingly lit from within. I watched, transfixed, as I was blinded by this blue light and shown how to see in a whole new way.

At the same time the blue light took over, a corresponding energy arose within me. Its intensity built steadily, inexorably, as if it would soon explode and blast my observing self into smithereens. That's really what this force felt like. Something in me gave over to the force, willing to be catapulted into a different dimension if that's what Spirit had in store for me. Yet just as there was a part of me coaxing this energy forward, another part, equally automatic, would act as a limiter switch. After about a minute or so of energetic surging, suddenly it would disappear in a flash, as if a plug had been ripped out. My eyes would clear and the energy would reset to zero. Then, after a few moments, the whole thing would repeat.

This push toward some new kind of seeing and being would run through about ten cycles before I found myself wakewalked out of the bathroom. It happened to me at least a dozen times. Only later did I learn that the blue light I saw was often associated with Kundalini illuminating the third eye, and that what I was drawn to do spontaneously was actually an ancient meditative practice called "mirror gazing."

Wherever the supernatural in me seemed to have a clear purpose, close by was a far more disorderly expression. This did not just occur in the sexual realm, as described in the previous chapter, but everywhere else as well. A few specific examples stand out. First, at a time when I was trying to decide whether to date a woman named Sarah or hold a candle for the erstwhile Hannah, I found myself wakewalked directly to my laptop. My fingers trembled over the keyboard, as if above a Ouija board, as if Spirit was about to make a proclamation. I waited, expectant, while the trembling continued for a minute or two.

Then, my fingers began to type. "You . . . should be . . . with Sarah."

There it was. Plain as day. Okay, I thought, there's my directive. So I remained transfixed at my desk, imagining how to move things forward.

But suddenly my hands began to tremble again. I let them do their thing as before, readying myself for another download. After about a minute, it came.

"You . . . should be . . . with Hannah."

Wait—what? I was totally thrown. How could opposing edicts be simultaneously valid? Of course they couldn't. After a while I tended toward the conclusion that the energy was toying with me. But why? Was there anything positive to glean from it?

One part of me wanted to take the whole experience as an indictment of the energy, to judge it meaningless at best and dangerous at worst. This potential conclusion harked back to the experience on the balcony, when I realized the energy had no intention or ability to protect me.

But another part of me saw the episode as a way for the energy to lay me low, to crush whatever elements of self-inflation still remained in my persona, similar to the way a flesh-and-blood guru might. From this perspective, the energy's manifestation as a trickster was the perfect guise. "Do you actually think," it seemed to say, "that the Source of the universe gives a shit who you date? What a fool!"

I considered myself dutifully humbled.

This same quandary about how to interpret conflicting guidance showed up in relationship to my health. Throughout my early years with Kundalini, it consistently wreaked havoc on my body. I haven't shared much about that here because there are many extensive accounts of such physical challenges. In my case they were mainly digestive, as if the energy's fire burned me up and dried me out. This increased my Chronic Fatigue–related

Irritable Bowel Syndrome (IBS) symptoms to an almost unbearable degree. I couldn't figure out what to eat, how much, or when.

One day the energy wakewalked me over to the refrigerator and opened it. In the same way my hands had trembled over the keyboard during the Sarah/Hannah event, they did so now over the shelves of food. Then they slowly removed a number of items, one at a time, and threw them aggressively into the trash. I appreciated both the clarity and seeming conviction of the process. "Okay," I thought once more, "I have my marching orders."

Yet, just a few minutes later, the entire thing repeated in reverse. With just as much emphasis, each item was retrieved from the trash and placed back on the refrigerator's shelves.

Admittedly, I was disappointed. I had so hoped for some valuable input. While I decided to take this as another humbling, it also really pissed me off.

In a rare willingness to address my frustration, or so it seemed, the energy next decided to lighten things up. Same point, different delivery. This comic turn occurred in a hotel room down the road from Rocket Science, where I holed up after a late night at work. Before heading back to the office the next morning, I sat upon the bed in meditation. After a few uneventful minutes, a booming voice issued forth from my mouth.

"Something wonderful . . . is about to happen."

This startled and delighted me. I remained in rapt attention, prepared for an inner event of great significance. After a few minutes the voice boomed forward once more.

"Something wonderful . . . has just happened."

If anything wonderful had indeed happened, I'd missed it! But how? Did I wait in the wrong way? Look in the wrong direction? Why wasn't it mine to behold?

Rather than respond with anger or disappointment, this time I just had to smile. I had fallen once again for pomp, for the tantalizing bait of a "special" experience that was all about me. Clearly, in that regard, I still had more work to do.

◆

Another part of living in two worlds was deciding how and when to bridge them. My first try, outside of sessions with Theresa, was with Hannah. Deeply sensitive, Hannah could immediately tap into the new energy once we spent a little time together, post-exorcism. Eventually, I let her see it's full force—with trembling, chanting, and gyrating included. We also let it lead us once when making love, as part of one of our many attempts at reunion. This provided the first inkling that things would change for me, sexually, when a partner joined with the energy and me (see next chapter).

Hannah's overall response was mixed. On the one hand, she reveled in the new dimensions the energy brought to me, and us. She met this with respect and awe that felt genuine and affirming. But she was also wary of it, if not downright suspicious. Once she referred to it, snarkily, as my "energy show." Over the years that followed, I experienced responses like this a few other times. I learned, therefore, to be cautious about when to share it and how.

Before arriving at such caution, I also found out what it was like to share the energy with someone who couldn't relate to it at all. Steven, my game design partner, had been there at the very beginning. I felt close to him in many ways and wanted to not hide anything from him. So while I knew better than to let the energy flow in his skeptical, atheistic presence, I did once try my best to describe what had been going on. Over dinner, with his fiancé, Elizabeth, I gave them a five-minute summary.

Afterward, they stayed quiet for a moment, then looked at one another strangely and sipped their wine. Steven said, "I have no idea at all what you were just talking about. The only word that meant anything to me was 'Shakti,' because that's the name of Elizabeth's cat." Needless to say, I kept mum with both of them after that.

Eventually, I also got to experience the opposite end of the spectrum. I shared the energy in meditation with my close friend Seth, who had spent years in the ashram of Adi Da and had many supernatural and energetic encounters of his own. As we sat together and the energy moved through me in its myriad ways, Seth received it quietly, reverently. It touched a place in him that resonated and responded in kind. He recognized its sacred source without either inflation or diminishment. His response was truly a balm to me.

Some aspects of bridging the worlds fell into place without any deliberation. One of them was how much time to let the energy run during my everyday schedule. For the first couple years of the awakening, this naturally averaged about two to four hours. With any less time spent in a surrendered state, the energy would back up inside me and create incredibly painful headaches, backaches, and the previously mentioned digestive debacles. If I gave more time to the energy, my fragile body would be overstretched like a rubber band, and I would experience a snapback of fatigue and inflammation that would sometimes take two or three days to reset. In the years that followed, the time necessary for the energy to take center stage would gradually and effortlessly decrease.

At no time, however, was there an option to deviate from the requirement of the moment. I remember reading, in Sylvia Boorstein's memoir, *That's Funny, You Don't Look Buddhist*, about her own encounter with Kundalini energy and the way it would cause her arms to suddenly flap about alarmingly in public places. Her way of dealing with this when it occurred was to purposely curtail her meditation practices for a while until the energy calmed down.

Whenever I experimented with such an approach, aiming to tamp down the energy even a little, things would quickly became more painful, chaotic, and adversarial. It helped me realize that Georg Feuerstein's warning against premature integration of the energy also applied to putting *any* limits on it that weren't absolutely necessary. What worked for Sylvia, alas, wasn't in the cards for me.

◆

While the supernatural realm continued to exert its demands upon me, so, too, did the prosaic world. I often found myself beset by common woes. One night I was heading home from the laundromat, nearing my exit on the interstate, when one car sideswiped another just in front of me. The offending driver fled the scene. The victim of the hit and run came to a halt, treacherously, in the center lane. I stopped about twenty yards behind and turned on my hazard lights to warn and slow the oncoming traffic. I helped the injured driver to the side of the road, where we waited together for the California Highway Patrol.

I sighed with gratitude when a patrol car soon came toward us with lights flashing, but my relief was premature. The lone vehicle in front of the CHP car didn't see my car's flashing lights in time. It plowed straight into my car at almost full speed. The impact of the crash dragged my car right into the sideswiped one. This compressed my car like an accordion. The glass of its rear hatch shattered, raining thousands of shards into all the laundry just below.

In the end, no one was seriously hurt. Other than the hassle of dealing with insurance and endlessly plucking glass from my clothes, I emerged from the ordeal unscathed. But what stood out for me at the time was how unperturbed I was by the whole event. I watched the big crash with calm curiosity. No anxiety, no adrenalin. It was as if my many recent spiritual emergencies had somehow inured me to earthly ones.

This placid acceptance of potentially traumatizing events played out three more times, each one very different from the others. The first was a health scare that began when I discovered a tumor the size of a softball that seemed to appear on my thigh overnight. At the biopsy, I begged the technician to take more fluid for fear of the result coming back inconclusive. She did take more than usual, yet my fear came to pass anyway. The doctor told me that my tumor was very likely benign, but not for sure. In the event of malignancy, this particular type of tumor was known to metastasize lethally to the lungs. So keeping it onboard was like living with a potential time bomb.

Still, I didn't hurry to excise it. I sensed intuitively that it was indeed benign. I also sensed that it wasn't a random mutation as the doctor surmised. I believed it was some kind of system overload from running so much Kundalini energy for a very long time (reminding me of Suzanne Segal and her *Collision with the Infinite*).

So I decided to shrink the tumor myself, if possible, using a Chinese medicine approach. Hannah taught me how to administer self-acupuncture, as well as the exotic practice of heating the points with a smoldering stick, known as moxibustion. Every day for six months, I spent a half hour on the deck of my apartment, poked and smoked, and succeeded in shrinking the growth perhaps by half. But there it still was, as if in a standoff, daring me to underestimate its destructive power.

Eventually I had the tumor removed, which itself turned into a crisis. The surgeon told me that it would be a simple procedure because he had "one-hundred percent visualization" and nothing was obstructing his path. That made sense. I trusted him.

What he didn't tell me was that his visualization included bones and muscles but not nerves. The tumor turned out to be nesting in a tangle of nerves that had to be torn apart for access. Following the excision, I was beset by an almost intolerable amount of nerve pain, as well surface numbness. The pain lasted many months. Nothing would relieve it. Some of the numbness remains to this day, twenty years later.

The final pathology report confirmed that the tumor was benign. This offered only an abstract consolation as I hobbled about, wincing and howling with each step, bitter at the false confidence my surgeon had projected. But bitterness aside, the whole ordeal affected me in a way similar to the totaling of my car. *Okay, so this is what's happening now*, I told myself. *Get really intimate with the pain, the limited mobility, and especially all the raw and vulnerable emotions it is bringing forth.*

That's exactly what I did. And in those moments when resistance surfaced, and I couldn't quite find that ability, I leaned into my lapse and welcomed that, too.

The second imperturbable response occurred during an event that otherwise might have been treacherous. I came home from a relaxing night at the movies, opened the front door and switched on the light. In front of me, frozen in shock, was a burly mama raccoon with her four babies in tow. Somehow they had figured out the pet door, just as that gangster tabby had months before, and were feasting on the contents of my own cats' bowls when I arrived.

In a split second, the baby raccoons raced back toward the pet door and escaped through it. But the mama, disoriented, ran upstairs to the second floor.

My heart pounded. Adrenalin did course through me this time. After all, I had a wild animal loose in my home that would likely attack if approached. At the same time, though, a kind of preternatural calm radiated through me. I didn't know in advance what to do, but the best course of action materialized nonetheless.

I swung the front door wide open to create an unmissable exit point. Slowly, almost as if wakewalking, I proceeded up the stairs. Once on the second floor, I saw the mama raccoon in one of the bedrooms, hanging frantically from a sliding screen door. She traversed it nimbly with her sharp claws, both vertically and horizontally, desperate to get outside. There was no chance of that, however, because behind the screen door was a locked glass one.

The raccoon heard me arrive at the top of the stairs and snapped its head around. We locked eyes. Taking slow, mime-like steps, I acceded her direct access to the stairs in a wide arc that took me to the far end of the hallway. Somehow, she got the message. Leaping off the screen door, ripping it in the process, she barreled toward the stairs, flew down them and was out the front door in a flash.

Since I didn't get to view her departure, I waited a few moments and then tiptoed downstairs to make sure she was gone. Then I locked the front door and the pet door as well. I let my breathing slow. I shook out the remaining adrenalin. Within a few minutes the whole experience shifted from terrifying to hilarious.

The third imperturbable response was to a situation that was anything but hilarious. The graphic adventure game I was codesigning at Rocket Science had such an unusually high budget that it garnered a lot of industry attention. As a result I was asked to speak on panels about interactive storytelling. Those appearances led to connections with other companies, and some of them hired me for projects of their own. One of those companies was Berkeley Systems, creators of the hit title, *You Don't Know Jack*.

I led the Berkeley Systems creative team in the development of a game prototype that aimed to weave many branching and intersecting narratives through the device of a telephone switchboard. It was a team effort, but the idea and implementation was my personal responsibility. After a couple of months, the prototype was ready for focus group testing.

As per the industry custom, a third-party company assembled a group of gamers to experience the prototype and share their views. The creative team watched this test from the other side of a two-way mirror. What transpired wasn't just a negative response, but a seemingly endless outpouring of disgust. The focus group hated every aspect of the game, from idea to execution. Their feedback wasn't reserved for the game itself, but also included its designers. One person actually said, "Whoever put this piece of crap together should be fired immediately and never allowed to make another game!"

On the team side of the mirror, I went beet red. I was mortified, humiliated. I felt all company eyes on me and knew that both the project and my gig designing it were total goners. Plus, there was nowhere to hide. I had to just stand there and listen as the savaging continued and the creative team distanced themselves from the fiasco and laid it all on me, the outsider.

So there I was, alone in my failure and shame for all to see. Never before had I been in such an extreme predicament. When faced with anything close to it in the past, I had always reacted defensively and attempted to rationalize away the vulnerability and hurt. This time though, with no conscious effort or intention, I found myself taking the opposite tack.

Wow, look at this, I thought with surprising curiosity. *You're in role of the culprit. What does that feel like?* It felt, I noticed, like a punch to the stomach by a fiery fist. I also noticed a surge of similar fire travel up my core and into my throat. My shoulders slumped and my chest caved inward. As I kept paying attention to these sensations, I also had a sensation of shrinking, shrinking, as if soon I would disappear.

But I didn't disappear. Neither, at first, did any of the emotions in my body. They pulsed, ebbed, and flowed like waves, but overall stayed incredibly intense. I excused myself and went to the bathroom. Before, this exit would surely have been a way to escape my torment. But now, without any distractions, in the privacy of one of the stalls, I connected even more fully to my body's trauma response. As a result, without willing it, the quality of my beholding shifted from curiosity to tenderness. I was wounded, no way around it, but also soothed.

After a few minutes, a quiet peace came over me. I was still raw, but also grateful for the chance to stay present with myself through the whole ordeal. I returned to the creative team and once again felt all eyes on me. I was no longer tense, but everyone else still was. They were also uncertain what to do or say. I could feel their edginess as if it were my own. Without thinking, I made a self-disparaging joke. I can't remember it specifically, but I do recall how it cut the tension, allowing everyone to relax in the knowledge that I wasn't about to freak out at them or myself.

All of this was possible, I concluded, because the trials of my awakening had rendered me much more able to weather emotional storms. Further,

I understood that every new experience, even the worst ones, offered its own unique opportunity to become more intimate with life. If I named and claimed them, and most important if I *felt* them, they would enrich rather than consume me.

◆

So . . . back to the original question. What kind of person was I becoming? To sum up: a more loving person. A person who shifted fluidly between the natural and supernatural. A person who was consistently humbled by his divinely unruly roommate. And a person who found himself meeting life's slings and arrows with much greater equanimity.

Beyond all that, though, or perhaps at the essence of it, I was inching closer to an edict that I'd first encountered as a teenager in the writings of the great exponent of Eastern philosophy, Alan Watts. The ultimate goal of spiritual life, Watts proclaimed paradoxically, was to be completely involved while at the same time totally detached. To witness your experience so fully that you become it.

Observe to merge.

Dispassionate passion.

Fervent serenity.

Impossible to understand, but sheer grace to taste.

12

As I continued to embrace and explore the paradox of living totally involved while completely detached, new qualities of the energy began to emerge. One of those qualities was the power to heal. I learned about this healing power by accident while spending an afternoon with my friend, Tara. We were catching up on her sofa when she told me that her back was tweaked from a recent bike spill. At the mention of her injury, the energy began to rise in me like it did just prior to wakewalking. Without mentioning anything about the energy (she didn't know about my whole Kundalini experience), I asked Tara if she wanted a brief massage.

When Tara nodded gratefully and laid down on the sofa, I knelt beside her, placed one hand on the small of her back, and waited to see what would happen. For about a minute, nothing. Then my hand began to move around her back as if in search of something. Best as possible, I ignored my analyzing mind and just observed what unfolded. Soon my hand landed on a particular spot and began to tremble. It seemed to tap into whatever was there and then intensify. The light trembling, just above Tara's skin, went on silently for a few minutes. As if responding to an unseen signal, my hand then lifted off the spot and joined my other hand in a spontaneous *Namaste*.

Tara turned over with a stunned expression. "How did you do that?" she asked.

"Do what?"

"That was the exact spot where all my pain was," she told me. "I didn't say a word about it. You found it, did your thing, now the pain is all gone." I explained a little to Tara about the energy, keeping things general and light. Without premeditation, I used the phrase "getting out of the way" to describe my only conscious participation in the process. To this day, that still best describes my personal part in any gifts the energy imparts to others. I feel its call, drop into fuller presence, let go of any will or volition, then surrender to whatever happens.

Over the months that followed, similar scenarios took place with other friends. Sometimes, in addition to the trembling hand, I found myself toning or chanting. I also began to whistle intermittently. It was a breathy whistle that felt vaguely shamanic, although I'd never visited a shaman, undergone any training, or even read a book on the subject.

Each time a new wave of chanting, whistling, toning, or trembling went through me during an impromptu healing session, a part of me would split off into self-consciousness. I'd wonder anxiously if the person with me would be put off or view my actions as an affectation. In spite of their seeming trust and receptivity, I'd brace myself for disapproving or dismissive feedback at the end.

Thankfully, that didn't happen. If my friends were new to such phenomena, they intuitively found it to be legitimate and trustworthy. If they were energy veterans, what arose in our sessions felt just right.

Every time these results came to pass, I'd heave a huge sigh of relief. My self-consciousness would subside just a little more. This growing comfort in sharing energy with others reminded me of that time years ago when Luisa, the acupuncturist, writhed on a massage table in the throes of her Shakti. At first I had doubted the whole scene. Then, at the outset of my own Kundalini, I was on just such a table amidst even stranger vibrations. From that moment forward I doubted no more. And now, in a further twist, I was also becoming the healer above the table.

I mentioned all of this once to Hannah and she said, "It's true. You are a healer now. If you want, you can print up cards and offer that service." I appreciated her framing of the experience, but instantly knew that I didn't want to make it official in any way. That just wasn't my path. So instead of intentionally pursuing opportunities to let the energy heal, I just waited for them to come informally.

Flashing forward for a moment, I recall a time in 2012 when I was teaching a small-group intensive on emotional connection at the Kripalu Center in Massachusetts. I had been working in this capacity for more than ten years by then, and was comfortable guiding the participants into deep, loving presence. But in this public realm, I had yet to let out any of my strange energetic manifestations. After all, that wasn't in the course description, and the emphasis was rightfully not on me but rather on how people could learn to heal themselves.

But then, I found myself working with a woman accessing great waves of trauma. Her pain was just below the surface and longing for release, yet something blocked it from coming fully forward. As always, I was respectful of such a limit and proceeded cautiously, incrementally. At the same time, my hand began to tremble. It felt insistent, like it knew what to do and needed to be included. I kept it out of sight for a few moments, but as the pressure grew within me I decided to see what happened.

"Is it okay if I come closer," I asked the woman, "and support you in moving the energy?" She nodded, open but uncertain.

With her permission, I brought my trembling hand a few inches from her diaphragm. I held it there for a minute or so as she breathed a little deeper and cried a little harder. Then the whistling came, too, and that seemed to summon forth the rest of her pain. In between rounds of whistling, I whispered to her softly, "Is this still okay?" She nodded, and we continued in this way for another ten minutes or so until, wrung out, she reached a quiet and peaceful shore.

The whistling stopped, my hand stilled. I announced a break and wondered how the rest of the group would respond to my unannounced healing flows. I waited for people to be confused by them, even triggered, or at the very least to ask me where they came from, what they were, or how they fit into the curriculum.

Surprisingly, not a single person in the group addressed the occurrence with me in any way at all. We proceeded together as if it had never happened, not burying it as something to avoid but more like something that had arisen naturally and was complete in itself. I suspected that since I let the energies come through without inner conflict on my part, the group could be relaxed about their inclusion as well.

Since that experience, the healing energies have come through with similar trembling and whistling from time to time in other workshops or private sessions. I never know when they'll come, or for how long. They always bring a gentle, sacred support to the person I'm assisting. They feel both miraculous and at the same time no big deal.

It's important to stress that nothing about these healing energies is unique, or makes me unique. There are countless gifted healers of many stripes that serve their clients in profound ways. Many of those ways, I'm sure, are far deeper and more powerful than what moves through me. Plus, as with all the most impactful aspects of the energy, its healing component clearly arose from realms so far beyond the personality that it doesn't even make sense to think of it as generated by a "me." On the other hand, not to mention and include this aspect of the energy's expression would be, in my view, a kind of unhelpful hiding.

Though I never chose to highlight these healing energies, either back when Hannah suggested it or in all the years later, I did come to welcome them in my daily life. It took a while to become clear, but eventually there was no denying that I had entered a kind of informal fraternity of the energetically open.

Indistinguishable at first from anyone else, members of this fraternity are familiar and comfortable with giving, receiving, and sharing waves of non-physical energy. We also have a kind of radar for one another and often reveal ourselves subtly. An ordinary moment of eye contact may linger for many seconds more. In that extended connection our energies click on and flow. The same thing may happen in a hug. Once linked, we may vibrate together silently. Or, we may share big breaths, tones, and sighs. We enter a deeply resonant union similar to the alien "mind melds" of science fiction. To us, however, there's nothing alien about it.

Since the healing aspect of this energetic exchange was the least familiar to me, I spent a lot of time reflecting on it. I wondered, in particular, about what has recently become known as "energy medicine."

Energy medicine is based upon the premise that healing in a non-physical way is a skill that can be learned, developed, and taught. Its proponents claim that trained healers can cure not just aches and pains, like I did, but also serious disease. Theresa, in fact, had been trained in just such a modality.

All of which causes me to wonder: Is there one healing energy or many? If there is more than one, do they work in similar or different ways? And most important, can they be guided by conscious human intention, or is "getting out of the way" the only actual approach that truly works? I came to practice what Zen calls "don't know mind" with these fundamental questions, but remain sure about one thing: I can never teach anyone else to access healing powers in themselves, because I have no idea how they work through me.

As a side note, I've sought out a wide variety of healers for decades, pertaining to my CFIDS, tumor, digestive issues, and a whole host of other ailments. I've persisted without experiencing much discernible benefit, even when practicing on myself. I let my intuition lead the way regarding which healers to trust and for how long. But I've noticed with a cautious eye how many use machines and monitors to proclaim with confidence what's actually happening. The machine may be as complex as a copper rod placed in the hand, connected to a big metal readout box. Or it may be as simple as a pendulum, or what's commonly known as "muscle testing."

What unites these approaches is seemingly external validation of whatever the process is supposed to be diagnosing or accomplishing. But the mechanism of that validation is almost always vague and impossible to confirm. How does a pendulum really work, for example? If it's determining the answers from within, why not just attune to one's own wisdom directly? Keeping such questions in mind, I gravitate toward healers who abide in mystery and don't need to offer concepts or devices to foster credibility. What made Theresa such a godsend to me, during the exorcism and beyond, was that her humility and uncertainty always remained front and center.

◆

Looking for additional emergent qualities of the energy brings me back, inevitably, to sex. Apart from a one-time encounter with Hannah, everything I've shared so far about sex has been between me and the energy itself. But in time I became ready to have sex again with other humans, which presented a new slew of questions and challenges.

You'll recall my experiment with mindful merging, in which the energy and I became one and the resulting ride was sexually ecstatic beyond description. Was that something that could be shared with another? I wondered. Would the energy want or even allow it? If so, what would be merging with what and who would be merging with whom? And most confounding of all, where would I find someone willing to engage in such a trial-and-error undertaking with me?

The last question, it turned out, was the easiest to answer. At previous transition points in my life, I had observed a wondrous phenomenon. Whenever I would find my way to greater healing and wholeness, I'd worry about having narrowed the pool of like-minded, suitable counterparts. But that worry was always unfounded, because what happened is that my "magnet" changed. After a few years of therapy, for example, I despaired at the possibility of finding women willing to share my new devotion to healthy intimacy. But whereas I had before never dated a person in therapy, now that was the only kind of woman who crossed my path.

Luckily, in reentering the sexual arena as a new being, the same phenomenon repeated itself. At one of the freestyle dances I loved to frequent, I found myself drawn to a woman who seemed both serious and joyful, and who moved with graceful abandon. We approached each other on the dance floor and began an improvised duet, circling one another, coming close then spinning apart without ever actually touching or speaking.

I returned the next week, hoping this woman would as well. She didn't, and I went home with an empty ache. Then the following week she came back, and we repeated our touchless, wordless dance. This time the energy between us increased, and we kept finding each other for ten-minute intervals, between dancing alone and with other partners. When the dance ended, I summoned up my courage and said hello while we were gathering our things. With the ice broken, and introductions made, Francesca and I walked out to our cars and into a yearlong relationship.

Francesca was a practitioner of tantric sex. She had been initiated by a previous boyfriend. I didn't know much about tantric sex when we met, but everything Francesca shared about tantra—altered breathing, spontaneous sounding, intense vibration, outrageous union, waves of whole-body orgasm—matched my experience of mindful merging with Kundalini. My magnet, fortunately, had shifted perfectly once again.

Much to my relief and delight, Francesca was open to the energy that was now inextricable from the rest of me, and to how it would impact our sexual connection. That didn't take long for us to discover, and it glued us together despite lots of other ways in which we were incompatible.

The first thing we learned together about sex with the energy is that it had a very specific and powerful interest in what happened between us. As I got out of the way, it surged forward. And in doing so, it ministered to Francesca in ways that I would have previously shied away from. What I did and said, how long or forcefully I persisted in any action—all of this would have been potentially transgressive to my pre-energy self. I'd brace myself for a conversation afterward in which Francesca would chastise me for being brutish, insensitive, and weird. And yet, in every single instance, Francesca's response was the opposite. She flowed in reverence with it all. My unfounded fear, and her corresponding appreciation, mirrored what had been happening during my above-mentioned attempts at energetic healing.

"How did you know that was the perfect spot, and the perfect pressure? What brought you to that pace and rhythm? Did you sense something that led you to back off and stop, just then, at the exact right moment?" She was both curious and wondrous.

I had no answer, except for my usual, "I just get out of the way." I came to see this new kind of sexual drive in me as wakesexing. I was aware the whole time, and could feel everything, but it was through my surrender to the experience that each action took shape.

Now, with another person involved, there was an additional component to such surrender on my part. It was often as if I could feel exactly what Francesca was feeling. My energy would rise in unison with hers. My excitement would derive not from seeking pleasure in my own body, but by eliciting it in her body. The energy locked into Francesca's response and sought to raise it, intensify it, explode it. *More, more, more!* That was its unspoken edict. The energy thrived upon Francesca's ecstasy in a way we both could access, and in a way that felt equally carnal and transcendent, sexy and spiritual.

Part of what made our pairing so fortuitous was that most of what we were doing together matched uncannily with the aims of the tantra that Francesca had learned earlier. It seemed obvious now that in addition to its new healing quality, the energy possessed a tantric quality as well. Over ensuing relationships, I learned that the energy would always seek to find a partner's specific sexual blocks or edges. It would meet the partner there and attempt to break through, similar to the way it had worked on my own barriers, but without all the chaos and confusion.

The more sexually and energetically open the partner was, the further the energy would go, and the more of an ecstatically altered state we would travel through together. On the other hand, if the energy was not able to create any significant sync with the partner's energy, and therefore was not able to ignite us in the process, it would quickly get frustrated and lose interest. At that point it always seemed best to move on from the relationship.

◆

To my great surprise and appreciation, Francesca had learned to surrender as well as I had. This rendered our sexual experiences truly sacred. Through this sacred connection, the energy would shift in new and surprising ways. The most basic change was around orgasm. While locked into Francesca's orgasmic response, the energy no longer cared about mine. It would purposefully, effortlessly stave off my orgasm in order to keep drawing it out, extending and deepening hers. Many times I wouldn't even orgasm at all, yet there was no lingering frustration or tension. I would feel just as sated and suffused in afterglow as if I'd had an orgasm.

At times with Francesca, the energy would build even more intensely than it did with me alone. It would initiate long periods of "charging breath," as described in Kundalini yoga practices. I would find myself roaring at the top of my lungs, trembling so fiercely I seemed about to pass out. The energy would sometimes rub, press, or tap a part of Francesca's body with a similar ferocity. Its fixation on those body parts always matched the chakras, focusing mostly on her heart center, throat, forehead and crown.

The most extraordinary new dimension of the energy would emerge not during sexual encounters between Francesca and me, but after. I would find myself lifted from the bed and brought to the Namaste pose. From there I would begin a kind of ritualistic chanting and dancing. Francesca would look on with both reverence and bemusement as if I were some combination of angel, shaman, and elf. The chants came out of my mouth with great conviction, with mesmerizing yet indecipherable words, and also with effortless overtones, like those from Tuvan throat singers. Hard as I tried, it's worth noting, I could never reproduce the resonance of those chants when not in a wakesexing trance.

During the year or so Francesca and I remained together, we learned out the Tibetan Buddhist tradition of "dedicating the merit." It's customary, when reaching a vital experience of wisdom or realization, to offer that merit toward the peace and happiness of others, especially those who suffer. The intent of this practice touched my heart. It felt akin to the combination of soaring bliss and grateful vulnerability that filled Francesca and I as lovers. So, routinely, we would dedicate the merit of our blessing at the close of each encounter.

Amidst all this blessing, over time, there also emerged a corresponding sorrow. Francesca came to miss the more personal kind of sex, without the brutish blast of the energy or the ego-shattering serenity of its aftermath. She was never unappreciative of those miracles, but still longed for romance, soft affection, adoration of herself as a woman, my woman, and not just a spiritual co-conduit.

I understood this lack between us completely, and I was empathetic to the sorrow it caused. But my hands were tied in addressing it, at least sexually. To connect with Francesca required that first and foremost, I become as present as possible. And whenever I dropped into presence, the energy would surge forth uncontrollably and take up all the space of me. My personal self, the one that knew how to adore the equally personal Francesca, was relegated to witnessing everything from the sidelines. Attempting to force that self forward while in sexual flow required a kind of shutting down, or shutting out, that was actually anti-presence, contorted and painful. Even when I did try, it didn't really work.

This lack of person-to-person sexual connection that plagued Francesca and me showed up similarly with other, future lovers. So did the same resulting sadness. It took over a decade for the energy and the personal me to blend more equally. Once that happened, on its own and without interference, it became possible for my partner to feel tenderness from me even while the energy ran full bore.

◆

From my time with Francesca onward, I intuited that the energy's emergence as both healer and lover overlapped. Together, they had the potential to offer profound sexual healing, a kind of radical wholeness both for me and my partners that embraced not just an unbounded self but the very entirety of creation. The one film I directed, a few years before the energy awoke, was actually called *Sexual Healing*. Somehow, although the film had nothing to do with Kundalini, it provided an uncanny foreshadowing.

Aware of what a gift sexual healing could be, I longed to share it, to guide others in their own pursuit of what Francesca and I had experienced together. As with the energy's *non*-sexual healing, however, I couldn't offer guidance about our unique brand of tantra because I had no idea how it happened. Again, getting out of the way was all I understood for sure. For some reason, though, I couldn't quite leave it alone in this realm. Might it be possible, I wondered, to help people get spacious enough in what their consciousness could hold, and free enough in what it could express, that their own version of sexual healing might materialize as well?

Many years later, I became a presenter at the International Conference on Sacred Sexuality. In my four workshops over two years, I did my best to distill the essence of what Francesca and I shared, and of what I continued to share with almost all my partners afterward. Here is a description for one of my conference offerings.

Diving Deep: How Sexual Energy Reveals Your Essence

What would sex be like if we shed all our principles and expectations about it? What if we approached sex with a totally naked mind?

In such a void, we're often able to explode the limitations of false identity and unite with our true Self. This true Self is beyond the distinction of masculine and feminine, you and I, or even I and All.

Instead of being made love to, *now we're made love* through. *In these moments, what roars between ourselves and our lovers are the deepest, wildest forces of creation. These forces can be summoned and honored, but not controlled. It's by learning*

to surrender to them that we realize, and actually experience,
our divinity.

Those four workshops, it turned out, were as far as I got as an official pre-senter in the tantric world. It never felt entirely natural to me. What did, and what I'll describe in more detail soon, was applying the same principles and practices in the confounding realm of emotions.

13

I can feel the end of our story

It's coming

And I know I haven't done us justice

Not even close

I would apologize except I know You don't care

Caring has never been Your thing

You push, provoke, confront, dare

There is no enough with You

Ever

You and Your creative destruction

Relentless

Merciless

Everything must be decimated in order to be recreated

Reseeded

Rebirthed

Not just by You but *of* You.

You reemerge from Yourself as us

To know yourself as never before

Evolution is too slow for You

You created it to throw us off Your scent

Nature's cycles are just numbing crumbs

If we knew the totality of Your devastation

We'd give up the ghost

If we knew the radiance of Your manifestation

We'd drown in awe

So You dumb it down

Dumb us down

Until You can't resist the urge to tweak

To get *personal*

And thus we met, You and I

Mortal to immortal

So You could blow me up from the inside

But to what end?

Was I just a detour

On the highway back to Yourself?

Or some kind of quality control?

Let's see how much the latest model can take

If he crumbles, no worries

Just melt him down for scrap

Commence once more

You've got all the time in the world

This is infinity, after all

But despite Your omniscience

One crucial thing escaped You

If I surrendered enough

Loved You enough

Then You, too, would be laid low

Knocked off your perfect perch

You'd take the hit

Absorb the blow

Become as wounded and flawed and scarred as me

Go ahead

Admit it

That's what happened, didn't it?

Our love mattered to You

I mattered to You

You couldn't extract yourself from what we became together

That's right

The Almighty fell in love

Just a little

Just one facet

But just enough

To become real

Tentative

Uncertain

Vulnerable

And when we found each other there

When we connected there

Combusted there

Something truly new was born

And our work was done

But then we still had time

To play

To serve

To dedicate the merit

To spread the Good News

Even if it's impossible to convey

Yet truth be told

I thought I could pull it off

That's on me

You would never dream of trying

Only I did

Still am

Even as I admit defeat

While somehow sure

After so many words

Futile words

That You find my doomed endeavor

Endearing

◆

After the focus group fiasco with Berkeley Systems, my possibilities for work as a game designer pretty much dried up. Soon, I knew, money would become tight and I'd need to figure something out.

My first choice for income was to return to Hollywood as a screenwriter. That meant creating a new script "on spec," and marketing it through one of my previous agents or managers. Having done this many times before, as the old me, I was curious about what it would be like to write from a post-Kundalini perspective, and whether I'd be able to bring a new kind of freedom and flow to the process.

Fittingly, given everything I'd been through, I chose to write an edgy comedy about the psychological idea of the shadow. I called it *Flipside*. The protagonist is good hearted, but also inhibited and ineffectual. Through some unexpected magic, his literal shadow separates from his body and comes to life as a double. This shadow-self possesses all the protagonist's

repressed power. At first it seems like an amazing ally, able to imperso
the protagonist, step into previously difficult situations, and totally kick ass
on his behalf. As a result of this borrowed verve, the protagonist begins to
triumph in both work and love.

However, soon it becomes clear that the shadow has a darker motive.
His aim is to trade places with the protagonist, to relegate *him* to the shadows. And so the story becomes a life or death struggle, with one key twist:
as expressed in Jungian psychology and related traditions, one's shadow can
never be destroyed without total, mutual demise. So in my tale, the shadow
must not be vanquished but instead integrated. The protagonist must find
a way to embody all the shadow's power and cunning himself. In usual
blockbuster style, this was meant to be accomplished with lots of grand
action and special effects.

I had an incredible time writing this piece. The process was fun—
exciting and freeing. It felt like I was becoming a better writer, less careful
and therefore more effective. My personal experience of writing *Flipside*
matched the protagonist's journey in a way that I relished.

Except, Spirit had other plans for me. The screenplay made the rounds
and didn't sell. Nor did it generate enough enthusiasm to get me back in the
game. So I found myself at a strange crossroads. On one hand I was without
a career, or even a career direction. I was also single at this point, and had no
ties to any particular person or community. I lived alone on the top of a hill
in Mill Valley, and often seemed to be floating, untethered, from life itself.

On the other hand, I felt radiantly alive, blissful even. A connection
to Source seemed available to me in almost every moment, and it became
easier and easier to return to Source at those times when my all-too-human
reactivity eclipsed me from it. As a result, I never actually felt apart. There
was nothing to be apart from, only a single whole out of which new facets
arose endlessly into view. I let myself collapse into every moment, and was

embraced by every moment in return. There was no problem, nothing to fix, and nothing in particular to do.

Amidst this delicious collapse, I wasn't compelled to reassert my personal identity, or to grasp for the illusion of solidity or control. And yet I still needed to be Raphael, to let Spirit express itself uniquely through me as it does through every other aspect of creation. Exploring how to do this in a practical way, I was drawn once again to Ken Wilber, who calls upon adepts to simultaneously behold the Relative and the Absolute.

The Absolute refers to the essential unity of all existence. I know, for example, that the tree outside my window is arising within the same *field of being* through which my eyes are seeing it. On an Absolute level there is no separation between us.

The Relative refers to the mysterious way in which such unity also manifests through infinite variation. From this vantage point, it's clear that I could cut down the tree and it wouldn't be there anymore, or that if I stopped looking at the tree it would continue to exist outside my subjective awareness. On a Relative level we are indeed separate—obviously distinct and different.

So just as we are truly one, we also appear incontrovertibly as two. Neither recognition cancels out or trumps the other. In fact, Ken Wilber teaches that attending to this fundamental paradox in everyday life is the mark of true spiritual sophistication.

Here's how that intention works for me. If I tilt too much toward a "we're all one" vibe, my life force becomes muted and mushy. If I tilt too much toward ego assertion, my life force becomes strained and strident. The sweet spot arises when I surrender to the unity of Spirit and let it illuminate the path of my singular expression. That way, we're in it together. This enables me, putting it another way, to see the entire fabric while being my individual thread.

Keeping this all in mind, up on my Mill Valley hilltop, I waited with pregnant patience for the next steps of my path to appear. For the most part, I remained free of fear or impulse. But still, the clock continued to tick. So I asked myself a very direct and specific question: *If I knew that I would be dead at the end of the next six months, what would I choose to do with this time?*

◆

The answer came to me in just a few days. I would write a book. That book would share the insights of my awakening experience with others. While it wasn't the time to tell the whole tale, as I've done here, I would focus on its fruits. I would use all the chops I could muster as a writer to present those takeaways as clearly as possible, without unnecessary jargon. I would make my principles and practices accessible to people, whatever their beliefs. I would ask them to take nothing on faith, and instead to test out my offering in the laboratory of their own lives.

I have no specific memories of the time in which that manuscript came to be. Overall, though, two things about it stayed with me. The first is that the process was truly gratifying. I felt a deep sense of purpose and an alignment with Spirit that allowed me, in this realm as with all the others, to get out of the way.

The second thing that I recall was a commitment to remain present as the manuscript took shape. It was crucial not to think about what would happen afterward, because otherwise my marketing background would have interfered and led to fatal compromises and dilutions along the way. So I reminded myself over and over to surrender the outcome—that all would be well whether the final draft shot up the bestseller list or remained unpublished in the attic.

The book took about six months to complete. After a round of revisions, I sent it off to a number of literary agents and continued to surrender the outcome. I was also now officially broke, so I split my days between tending to the energy and looking for work. My job experience in Hollywood and new media rendered me uniquely overqualified for almost anything suitable. But I surrendered the outcome in this pursuit as well, endlessly tweaking my resume and purposely underselling my credentials. I must have applied for hundreds of writing gigs, both freelance and salaried, without landing a single interview.

Then I received a call from an online start-up named carclub.com. Their mission was to replace the venerable "triple A" with a more nimble online version. The callback made no sense, since I was definitely not a car guy and could barely remember applying. I set up a phone interview almost as a lark, and also because it was the only response I'd received. I kept playing along with the seeming charade through a round of in-person interviews, waiting for them to realize their mistake. But somehow, perhaps because of the freewheeling ethos of the dot-com bubble, they offered me a full-time job as a copywriter in their marketing department

"You may ask yourself / How did I get here?" Those Talking Heads lyrics were a constant refrain in my mind as I became an official carclub.com working stiff. The daily commute by car and ferry to the South of Market district of San Francisco felt surreal. The office was just a stone's throw from the now-defunct Rocket Science Games, which added to my sense of dislocation, and also induced a sharp longing for the days when my storytelling input was sought after and appreciated.

Still, I kept my head down and did whatever was asked. I spent most of my time coming up with quippy headlines for internet banner ads. I took solace in recalling how the beat poet and fellow Reed College alum, Lew Welch, made money in a similar way and was renowned for coming up with perhaps the greatest advertising slogan of all time, "Raid kills bugs dead."

All this, I told myself, was my contemporary version of "chop wood, carry water." For the most part I remained willing and grateful. No one at carclub.com knew of my entertainment industry credits or, especially, about my ongoing travails with the energy.

The one thing they did know about was my Chronic Fatigue Syndrome, which was impossible to hide because of my mandatory post-lunch collapse. Due to the Americans with Disabilities Act, the company was obliged to find me a dark and quiet resting place. The best they could do was the server closet, so each afternoon I would retreat there for my necessary but non-restorative downtime.

On a thin pad, surrounded by whirring, flashing computers, I would alternate between actual sleep and the familiar, unavoidable waves of Kundalini. Those waves would send my body into fits of rapid breathing and jerking spasms. Though I was just inches away from the rest of the staff, my oddities were completely undetected behind the locked door.

When my phone alarm would go off, I'd return blearily to my desk as if back from a conventional power nap. No one ever said anything to me about this directly, but I did overhear periodic grumblings. A few of my coworkers wondered if my diagnosis was a ruse, designed to get what they should have coming to them also.

Be careful what you wish for, I imagined myself replying if anyone ever asked.

◆

After a few months of chopping wood/writing headlines at carclub.com, my agent called to let me know that there was a buyer for my book. The offer wasn't for very much money, so I'd have to keep working, but the publishing schedule would be accelerated and the release date would be less than a year away.

This news was thrilling, and it landed in me as a soft affirmation of the path I had chosen. I recognized that the time before publication was immensely valuable. It allowed me to shift gradually into marketing mode, while at the same time squirreling away the savings I'd need for a suitable launch.

I spent these prepublication months wrestling with the tension between the life I was living and the teachings I was about to offer. The book was a manual for practicing presence. Its strengths, I hoped, were clarity and accessibility. In other words, my primary aim was for it to make sense. But my daily existence didn't make much sense at all. While I gamely played out my roles in the realm of consensus reality—employee, soon-to-be author—the energy still continued to have its way with me.

I would slip into altered states with no warning. It could happen at my desk, in the gym, or while watching TV. Like a light switch toggling on, suddenly the energy would flood my awareness. It would take me, if I let it, sometimes for just a moment and other times for hours. But no matter how wild or confounding the flood, I never lost connection with my awareness. These were still conscious trances, like the ones I've described earlier. They didn't feel like the illusory "fireworks," those spiritual temptations and distractions I'd been warned about so often. To the contrary, they felt as significant as they did mysterious.

Around this time I came across the confirming perspective of William James. In an essay titled *The Hidden Self*, he wrote:

> My own impression is that the trance-condition is an immensely complex and fluctuating thing, into the understanding of which we have hardly begun to penetrate, and concerning which any very sweeping generalization is sure to be premature. A comparative study of trances and sub-conscious states is meanwhile of the most urgent importance for the comprehension of our nature.

Later, this view was further buttressed for me by Etzel Cardeña, a Swedish psychologist who specializes in "anomalous psychological experience." Cardeña, as reported by the *New Yorker* magazine's Rachel Aviv:

> . . . has done research on altered states of consciousness in religious practice, and he found that some people who would otherwise be given a diagnosis of dissociative disorder have been able to channel their tendencies into rituals of spirit possession, trance, speaking in tongues, or intimate experiences of God. He said, 'There is a cultural context for surrendering themselves. It's not about getting rid of the dissociative state so much as giving it a syntax, a coherence, a social function.'

That's exactly what I was trying to do!

It's what I expressed in my own words at the end of chapter 7. But back then, in 2000, I didn't have the words for it, or the understanding, or the courage to share it all. So instead I settled for a dual existence. I straddled the physical and spirit worlds privately while portraying a more palatable persona publicly.

For the most part, this worked. But every once in a while the public persona would crack, and sometimes to comic effect. One such occurrence, etched in my memory, took place when a lengthy energy surge left me with painful muscle spasms all the way from my neck to my hips. It was just too much. I needed immediate relief.

"Hello?"

"Hi, I live in the neighborhood and could really use a massage. Do you have any openings this afternoon?"

"Yes, there's one with Derek at 3:00. Would that work?"

"I think so. But I have a condition. When someone massages me I can't stay silent or still. It often gets really loud and I don't want to disturb the other customers, so I'm wondering if you have a room that's pretty soundproof, and if Derek would be okay with lots of 'releasing.'"

"Hang on, let me check . . . Thank you for holding. Yes, Derek says, 'No problem' and we've got a really private room for you."

"OK, thanks, see you in a bit."

Grateful for the opportunity, I got dressed creakily and drove down to the studio. It was on the second floor, overlooking the Mill Valley town square. Derek met me graciously and led the way to a small cubicle away from all the others. I reconfirmed that he was okay with outward expressions of the energy, and then we got to work.

It was a great massage. I was able to surrender to Derek's touch as well as to the energy's roar. And "roar" is really the right word, because at times the volume of my spontaneous chants were nearly deafening.

Afterward I felt so much better, and practically bounded downstairs to the town square. It was then that I happened to look up, and noticed the location of the cubicle where my massage had just taken place. I also noticed a wide open window that neither Derek nor I had spotted during the previous hour. Which meant, of course, that all my attempted discretion had been for naught and that the whole town had been unintentionally blasted.

Around the same time, in seeking support for my almost-daily Kundalini challenges, I was delivered another comic blow. Since the very beginning of the journey, I had been grateful for my ad hoc team of guides and healers—Martin, Theresa, Rebecca, Zan, Georg Feuerstein, Derek, and others. I needed them because the energy's own direct guidance continued to prove erratic and unreliable. But what I truly longed for most was a teacher who understood the energy from the inside out, who could tame it, and tell me exactly what to do.

I heard from a friend about just such a teacher. He was a guru actually, and lived only a few hours away in the hills outside Santa Cruz. Once every few months, this guru would hold brief private audiences, both with his current disciples and prospective ones. All I had to do was get there, wait in a long line, and then present myself. The result might not be straightforward, I was warned, since the guru had stopped talking decades ago and communicated only via a hand-held chalkboard. This struck me as odd, yet a minimal eccentricity to accept in exchange for what I sought.

Soon I got myself to the ashram, and waited in line with great anticipation. After a couple of hours, my time arrived. I was ushered into the guru's chamber. I bowed, described my predicament, and humbly asked for any insight he could offer.

When I looked into the guru's eyes to join him in presence, he quickly turned away. Instead of meeting my gaze, he wrote on his chalkboard.

"What kind of work do you do?"

"I'm a screenwriter." He took in this information and wrote again.

"What movies have you written?" I told him this as well, while wondering why that would matter. But the guru's interest seemed piqued. He leaned forward intently, and wrote on the chalkboard once more.

"Do you have an agent?"

I did a double take. Realizing he was serious, my heart sank. This supposed master, the answer to my prayers, was actually soliciting *me* for Hollywood connections.

As soon as this sunk in, I politely redirected our exchange toward Kundalini.

"I know a lot about Kundalini," he scrawled. "But I'm not going to tell you about it now."

"Oh. Why not?"

"For that you'd have to move here and become my disciple."

I nodded soberly. I let out a sigh. I said I'd think about it.

To this day, for better or worse, no true Kundalini master has ever crossed my path. Does such a person actually exist? I have no idea.

Or, maybe now I do. While putting the finishing touches on this book, I was fortunate to make a connection with Joan Shivarpita Harrigan. Joan was initiated and trained as a Kundalini guide by her teacher and mentor in India, Swami Chandrasekharanand Saraswati. Together, in the mid-'90s, they founded Patanjali Kundalini Yoga Care (PKYC) in Tennessee and India. The service provided a place for people with Kundalini process to come for retreats and to receive precise guidance regarding their unique challenges.

The Swami and Joan offered a perspective on not just one but many types of Kundalini risings. Their perspective is far more comprehensive and profound than any I've ever come across. Trouble is, I didn't know about it during the days of my urgent need. And, by the time I did learn about it, the Swami had died and Joan needed to suspend working with new applicants. (The service does continue, however, through Silvia Viryanand Ebryl in Austria and India.)

Joan's two books lay out their approach with great precision. Her first is *Kundalini Vidya*, the second is *Stories of Spiritual Transformation*. After acquainting myself with Joan's work, I prevailed upon one of her students whom I happened to know to inquire whether Joan might be willing to review and comment on my manuscript.

Much to my delight, Joan agreed. After she read the draft, and took copious notes, we connected by Skype for a lengthy conversation. Initially I was worried that, with such an exhaustive system of Kundalini classification, Joan would be dismissive of my rude and chaotic awakening. What if she thought it wasn't even Kundalini at all, or that something had gone horribly wrong?

Instead, Joan began by expressing how moving she found my journey. There were actual tears in her eyes from the sacred awe with which she held each and every awakening, and the awakening process overall.

Joan saw my relationship with Kundalini as lifelong. "You came in with it," she said. "Your process was already existent at birth. Its ripening into active process indicated a karmic continuity piqued by intense romantic grief. Previous deep impressions arose, and Kundalini Shakti pressed you to do deep inner work to find a spiritual solution to your dilemma."

One significant outcome of this perspective, Joan explained, was recognizing that my mysterious chronic fatigue symptoms could actually be an effect of Kundalini on my energy system, even though its onset came before my energetic explosion in 1996. That hypothesis feels intuitively right, even though there isn't any way to test it.

Another crucial contribution from Joan is that Shakti, the divine within, is in charge of the whole Kundalini process. Joan explained to me that Shakti uses her energy, called prana, for her purpose of advancing spiritual progress. Within this framework, the energy itself isn't divine, but rather a tool that the divine employs in guiding each person's awakening.

Joan suggested that so many of my outlandish and concerning symptoms, like the slapping of my head and body early on, could be seen as Shakti trying to move the energy through the blocks within my inner channels.

Hopefully, Joan told me, we are able to develop a partnership with Shakti in co-managing the unfolding. When our most evolved and discerning selves can express through that partnership, the process unfolds as smoothly as possible. In Joan's view, the story I've told in this book is a testament to my own often confounding but ultimately hard-won version of that partnership.

Had PKYC been available to me in the wake of my energetic explosion, according to Joan, she would have encouraged me to "stop doing life" for a while and to dedicate myself as much as possible to supporting Shakti's mission. (This echoed what Theresa had mentioned would happen to someone having experiences like mine in many non-Western cultures). Joan and the Swami would have offered specialized physical, breathing, and meditation practices along with some lifestyle considerations. Most important, they would have recommended that I "spiritualize" the experience, meaning relating to it as a truly sacred unfolding, even when it seemed anything but, and focusing on a refined, virtuous approach.

Joan pronounced me a "Jnana yogi with a big heart," meaning that my mental faculties had been corralled in service of love, and that I used focused discernment to navigate my way through the process. She expressed that while all Kundalini processes continue to evolve, and very few are ever really done, my Kundalini rising had succeeded in its central function.

Some parts of Joan's interpretation feel spot on. About other parts I'm not so sure. Overall, though, my response to the encounter was one of great gratitude to both Joan and the Swami. I felt seen and supported in ways that I'd always longed for. I was welcomed fully as a member of their community. I belonged. I had a home outside of time and space, even though I never engaged with it directly.

14

The buyer for my manuscript was a small spiritual press named Quest Books. The most appealing part of the deal was a proclamation from the head of the company, whom I'll call Susan, that she loved the book as it was and didn't plan to change anything substantial before publication.

But almost as soon as the ink had dried on the contract, Susan reversed course and announced that we needed to change the title. The title I'd given the book was *Living the Questions*. This was an homage to the great mystical author, Rainer Maria Rilke, who is also the source for this book's epigraph. In *Letters to a Young Poet*, Rilke wrote:

> Be patient toward all that is unsolved in your heart and try to love the questions themselves, like locked rooms and like books that are now written in a very foreign tongue . . . The point is to live everything. Live the questions now.

Living the Questions was also the name I gave to a process for staying present at difficult times. This process was the centerpiece of the book, which made the title even more fitting. When my agent relayed the news of Susan's about-face, I was stunned. Disappointed. My first response was to say, simply, "No. That's not going to happen."

My agent patiently explained that it was important to be a team player, and that as a new author it behooved me to win the enthusiasm of not just Susan but of the sales manager as well. If they both thought the title would hinder getting the book into stores, that was something to seriously consider.

As I sat with the issue, different values within me vied for supremacy. Teamwork, yes, but also my vision, my truth. Healthy detachment, too, as well as listening, and respecting the wisdom of others. All those values mattered to me, and I couldn't figure out which ones to apply, or in what way.

Amidst the confusion, my agent called to say that Susan had backed down. If I remained adamant about my title, I could have it. Though irritated and deflated, she wouldn't stand in my way.

That moment marked a crossroads. If I could have remained strong and clear enough in my conviction, the book would have entered into the world just as I'd envisioned it, titled in accord with its own nature. In some parallel universe, perhaps, that's what happened. And in another one, maybe, I stuck to my guns, was willing to eschew publication in the short run to ensure integrity in the long run, and looked for another buyer.

Instead, in this universe, an old wound of unworthiness took hold. So, too, did my corresponding need to prove that I'm a "good boy." As a result, hoping in vain for a win-win, I began proposing other titles to Susan. She quickly pounced on my lack of resolve, and the momentum swung toward capitulation.

Because the book contained a lot about bliss, and new ways to embody that term, Susan deflected my initial alternative titles and lobbied to just call the whole book *Bliss*. That seemed impossibly flat to me, and unappealing, so I countered with *Unconditional Bliss*, since I'd never heard those words paired, and since they did reflect the book's assertion that our greatest happiness is available apart from any specific circumstances.

Susan agreed, but was still bitter. I was a little bitter, too, so the compromise didn't fully clear the air. Nor did it end up helping launch the book. Despite his confidence with the new direction, the sales manager didn't come close to meeting his own goals. Plus, Susan secretly told the book's designer to make the word "bliss" dominate the cover, and the word "unconditional" really hard to see. To this day, when I'm at a speaking gig, the person introducing me often holds up the book spontaneously, glances at the cover, and lauds me as the author of *Bliss*. I smile politely and cringe within.

Something more significant also came out of this skirmish around the title. That word, "bliss," for many people was just too New Age-y. After years of hearing Joseph Campbell's edict, "Follow your bliss," people turned away from the term as a lightweight cliché, redolent of false promise. Ironically, I'm one of those people. So months later, as I shepherded the book into the world, it was with a combination of excitement and apology.

I wanted to reach out to all the serious spiritual practitioners, and to the rightly skeptical. I longed to tell them, "Ignore the title. Please! The book was supposed to be called *Living the Questions*. I swear, you can take me seriously. If Rilke were alive, I know *he* would."

I'm including this story because it points to a crucial aspect of my awakening, and to awakening in general. After the blast of realization subsides, the personality definitely remains. So do any unhealed wounds, and the complexes they engender.

Even though I could seem "like a totally different person" as my mentors Thomas and Joanne had reflected, and even though I took my therapist Rebecca's advice to continue on the path of psychological growth, it was still painfully easy for me to get caught in my own traps. I still had, and always will have, lots more inner work to do.

Awakened or not, every human on the planet, no matter how lauded, successful, or seemingly self-realized, is still unavoidably fragile and flawed. When any teacher claims otherwise, in my view, it's a sure sign to run for the hills.

◆

Uh-oh.

He really thinks he's almost done.

Just a few more elements to include.

That can't be!

It's not enough!

He's just scratched the surface.

Hypocrisy monitor here—

Weren't we the ones who tried to stop him in the first place?

Yes, of course, but that was before.

We failed.

Now he's failing.

Does he actually believe that this comes close?

That he's doing justice to what we've all endured?

Martyr monitor here—

This was never going to be about hardship.

He never sought pity or commiseration.

Doing justice to what we've endured is no decent benchmark.

Okay, fine.

Then doing justice to the mayhem and magic and mystery.

Is that a decent benchmark?

Hasn't he botched that, too?

Yes. He has.

Let's just take a deep breath.

Sit with that for a moment.

Remember:

"I apologize in advance for the colossal failure this will inevitably become."

Yeah, he did say that. But who is this speaking, anyway?

We don't recognize you.

Sorry, I'm new here.

Tranquil.

Words aren't usually my thing.

Fine. So what's your point?

My point is that there's no problem.

There's nothing to worry about.

Nothing to fix.

In the realm of the Absolute, sure.

But everything's Relative here.

This book has to matter.

It has to succeed!

Are you certain?

What if its fate is inevitable?

What if you can't will it to be otherwise?

It's not about will.

It's about work.

Clearly, we need to work harder.

So go away. Leave us alone.

No—hear me out.

Consider, just for a moment, that you can relax.

That trying isn't going to make this better.

And that not trying *just might.*

Well . . .

Intriguing.

Tell us more about this not trying.

◆

Before writing the above dialogue, I lit a ritual candle with two outsize wicks. Right at the "tranquil" part, the smoke alarm went off. First, I flinched. Then I had to laugh. The piercing beep was like a waking dream with an obvious interpretation. The lack of an emergency, to the most vigilant, survival-focused part of my consciousness, can seem like an even bigger emergency.

◆

Fragile and flawed, intending to blend the Relative and the Absolute in a co-creation with Spirit, I set about exploring how best to present myself to the world once *Unconditional Bliss* came out. It's important to consider, in the personal growth arena, that authors largely craft their own personas. The first conclusions I reached about crafting mine were mostly about what *not* to do.

Don't claim expertise

I had no licensing or advanced degrees related to the work. I wasn't certified in any modality and didn't hail from any specific tradition. Leaving the expertise issue unaddressed would create tension from the outset. Much better, I decided, to get ahead of it. As a result, I planned to always highlight the book's second chapter, "Don't Believe a Word I Say." This allowed me to position myself as a fellow traveler, not an expert, which was actually in keeping with how I truly did see myself.

In addition, I decided to begin my presentations whenever possible with a joke adapted from Steven Wright: A guy goes into a bookstore and asks the clerk, "Can you direct me to the self-help section?" "Well, I could," the clerk replies, "but . . . wouldn't that defeat the purpose?"

Don't pose as a guru

A guru is anointed by a specific spiritual lineage. He or she teaches that lineage's followers as a realized being. While I didn't belong to a lineage, I *was* presenting principles and practices sourced from my own awakening. Still, I didn't see myself as a realized being or want to encourage possible projections upon me as a spiritual authority. Awakening, in my view, is by its very nature an always-evolving, never-completed process.

The way out of the guru realm, I concluded, was to echo the Buddha and implore people to trust their own direct experience. If my principles and practices were of service, great. If not, they could easily be set aside. And the best result of all, in my view, would be for people to customize my offering in whatever way worked best for them.

Don't pretend to be original

From the outset, it felt crucial to acknowledge that my core process for practicing presence was nothing new. In fact, it was the open secret at the mystical heart of all the world's great wisdom traditions. Though the expression of that secret changes across eras, cultures, and individual voices, its essence remains the same. A contemporary author such as me, therefore, can only hope to do it justice.

Another counter to presuming originality, I realized, could come from referencing the near-universality of the "dark night of the soul." I decided that whenever talking about my own dark night, out of which the awakening was born, I would also ask the people in attendance if they had ever experienced a similar dark night. I have continued asking that question to this day and, without fail, nearly everyone's hands go up.

Don't focus on the fireworks

There was no way to avoid mentioning my awakening, at least in very broad strokes. It's what led to the book's underlying contention: that one's ultimate peace and well-being is available in every moment, regardless of circumstance. That's the *what* out of which came the *how* of the Living the Questions process. And, since my awakening was spontaneous and unbidden, I did have to reference the sheer grace of it.

But in order to avoid a backlash from pointing out that grace, I developed a qualifying follow-up that would usually go like this:

"I recognize that it's a bit risky to talk about my experience in this way. There may be people in the group now wondering, 'Hey, where's *my* grace?' They may feel like something's lacking from their lives, and that this lack precludes their own awakening. Such a conclusion is actually the opposite of what I'm trying to express.

"It's equally important, therefore, to note that the great gift of my experience wasn't any of the seemingly special or exalted aspects. It also wasn't about developing spiritual powers or abilities. In the end, what truly mattered was the opening of my heart. And all our hearts open in different ways. Some people get there so gradually that the shift is nearly imperceptible. Which, in fact, can even be preferable, since in a case like mine your whole life gets turned upside down and you have to reinvent yourself from scratch."

As I write this, I'm aware that it might come across as too careful or calculated. Why not, instead, stop trying to control everything and just let it unfold? While I don't believe that there's one best way to present spiritual teaching, we've all seen so many instances in which a teacher's heedless, flamboyant presentation has been disastrous. Instead of spreading the "dharma," or spiritual truth, it has led to a cult of celebrity for the teacher at the price of confusion and pain for many followers. Therefore, I was passionate in my desire to avoid such confusion and pain, even if it sometimes might mean overcompensating.

It's only now, decades later, and for all the reasons previously described, that focusing on the fireworks became vital for different reasons.

Don't cultivate a mystique

Apart from direct claims of mastery or authority, there are many subtler aspects to the way teachers choose to present themselves. Each choice comes with cues, often unconscious, about how members of the audience or group are meant to perceive the one on stage.

In describing this, let me start with two small, seemingly trivial examples. First, I once found a custom-made linen shirt on Granville Island in Vancouver, BC. I just loved this shirt. It had an especially thick weave and big, round, metal buttons. The first time I wore it, at one of my early retreats, someone called out lightheartedly, "I love your guru shirt!" I instantly contracted. I hadn't realized it would send that signal. I definitely didn't want to be eschewing guru status with my words, on one hand, while on the other hand slyly promoting it. From then on, I wore the shirt rarely. And if I did wear it, I'd make sure to poke fun at it straight away.

Second, at many of the retreat centers where I held early events, participants sat on floor chairs called "backjacks" and augmented them with stiff pillows. Because of posture issues, I needed two or three pillows beneath me rather than just one. Even if trivial, or unnoticed, this had the possibility of sending a signal that I was somehow above the group. In order to counteract this perception, I would always point it out with a smile, and an assurance that I was a slightly elevated due only to a spinal condition.

If the mood encouraged it, I would also recount a brilliant comedy bit by the late Andy Kaufman. As a frequent guest on TV talk shows, Kaufman noted that the host always sat just a little higher than the guests. To poke fun at this sly power move, he constructed a talk show stage of his own, with his host's chair about *ten feet* above the guest's. He then peered awkwardly downward during the proceedings, conducting the entire interview as if nothing unusual was occurring.

Beyond shirts and pillows, many beloved teachers employ carefully orchestrated techniques to influence the participants at their events. Tony Robbins takes the stage to loud, thumping music. He creates hypnotic communal uplift as a rock star for human potential. Eckhart Tolle creates a similar effect with an opposite approach, speaking in an unusually soft, slow drone. These methods of delivery can be double-edged swords. While helping to open minds and encourage transformation, they can also shift focus from the message to the messenger.

Personally, I've always been wary of such delivery methods. Some of that has to do with my Jewish upbringing, and its emphasis on modesty. Some of it comes from my own allergy to "fronting," which was aided by Martin and all his knowledge of dark doings behind the scenes. This skepticism may also be related to my own limitations. I'm much better one-on-one, and in small groups. While I may sometimes long for a powerful stage presence, for an irresistible charisma that captivates the masses, those qualities just weren't in my cards.

To be such a spiritual star seems to require more than just innate capacity. It also usually requires a willingness to be seen that way, and to participate in the relationship which stardom engenders. Take Amma, for example, otherwise known as "the hugging guru." People all over the world wait in line for hours to receive one of her brief hugs. The presumption is that there's something different, more special about a hug from Amma than from anyone else.

I have no opinion about whether that's true, nor have I had the chance to see for myself. What interests me about Amma, in the context of cultivating a mystique, is that she doesn't just take part in these hugathons but actually organizes and promotes them. As far as I know, she doesn't deconstruct the dynamics of the situation. She doesn't point out or discourage projection from those staking so much on her exalted embrace.

All of this makes me even more curious about how she relates to the loving energy that passes through her. Does she view herself as a conduit or a bestower? Is she okay with the mystique that surrounds that loving energy? How does she respond when throngs of huggers make their experience specifically about her?

Having lived with the energy in me for more than five years by the time my book was nearing publication, I knew for sure that it didn't come from me. Neither did it belong to me. Therefore, when planning to go public as a teacher, I also knew that I couldn't let my gatherings be about me. I took it as a sacred task to dissolve projection, to keep doing my personal work and to talk about it as well. Otherwise, the impact of my offering would be tainted, and I'd be the one responsible.

I also saw how projection was insidious and could re-form like the Terminator. If not vigilant, I could inadvertently court a new round of projection as someone special, ironically, for how much I claimed not to be. To avoid that trap, I set out to portray myself as flawed and fragile, but in no way outstandingly so.

Around this same time, I often attended *satsangs*, or "gatherings in truth," with teachers from the nondual tradition who focused on the fundamental union of the perceiver and that which is perceived. One teacher I loved especially was Gangaji, a Bay Area acupuncturist who had experienced a spiritual awakening in India. Gangaji's own teacher, Papaji, selected her to help carry on the tradition. It was exciting to sit with Gangaji because she radiated authenticity. She guided her satsang attendees to welcome their emotional pain in a way that was both gentle and powerful.

And yet, it troubled me a little that Gangaji sat in front of the group in a throne-like seat. She was whisked on and off stage by attendants. I found myself more interested in what happened in her world before and after the satsang. How did her awakening change the way she dealt with life's thorniest challenges in real time, in real life?

By all accounts I've come across, Gangaji was and still is a wonderful, awakening being. But my questions about the delivery of her message shaped the way I decided to deliver mine. After a few early experiments with the satsang format, I decided not to teach that way. Instead, I soon opted for the workshop model, and positioned myself less as a leader and more as a facilitator. I did my best to avoid all fronting, and invited participants to join me in a sacred circle of vulnerability.

These choices turned out to fit me really well. They also served as a magnet for people most suited to my approach. Eventually, in 2014, I took that approach even further, creating the aforementioned Web interview series *Teaching What We Need to Learn*, in which I asked forty-five renowned leaders in personal growth and spirituality to share their own "growing edges." (http://teachingwhatweneedtolearn.com/listen) Getting those leaders to share as openly as possible required that I prime the pump with plenty of my own revelations. It's not an exaggeration to say that listeners to the whole series came to know the current, post-Kundalini me better than my family of origin.

◆

Back in the fall of 2000, when *Unconditional Bliss* was about to be released, I realized with a shock that all my careful preparations for how best to present myself were entirely conceptual. I had never given a single talk on the book's principles and practices. I hadn't yet experimented with the satsang format. I had never held a single workshop.

Most personal growth authors wrote their books as a capstone to years of teaching. They had *earned* their place. What if I, by contrast, was just a poser? What if my book worked only for me and not for other people? What if they didn't like my style? Was I about to face a crash and burn of my own doing?

Following the book's Living the Questions process, I asked myself:

What is happening right now?

I feel lightheaded, with a pit of fear in my gut and some shakiness in my limbs.

Then I asked the companion question:

Can I be with it?

The *yes* that came softly, yet confidently, allowed me to surf those sensations with my up-close and relaxed attention. After a few minutes, the waves of sensation within me crested and receded. In their wake I felt more calm, peaceful, and clear. I had let go of my resistance to any eventual outcome. Whatever happened with the release of the book, I was ready to continue "being with it."

From that place of renewed presence, I saw the need to do an informal focus group with people who would be likely readers of the book. The sting of my recent focus group disaster at Berkeley Systems gave me pause, but the accuracy of its outcome outweighed the pain I'd endured. I asked my friend Seth, with whom I had shared the energy in one my first person-to-person experiments, to seek out some participants from his extensive collection of Bay Area kindred spirits. Five of them, plus Seth and me, gathered one evening in my small Mill Valley apartment.

First, I introduced them to the book's main principles and practices. Next, I guided them in using the two questions to become more connected to their bodies and to the moment at hand. Last, I had them work together in pairs to address a pressing issue or challenge in their lives, using the two questions to move from resistance to acceptance in order to free up their perspective and approach.

To my great relief, the process was a big hit, scoring its main points for combining doing and being, practicality and spirituality. The gathering also allowed me to test-drive the way I presented the material in a workshop context, and to fine-tune the order and precise instructions for the exercises.

In the aftermath of that first trial run, I understood another aspect of its momentousness for me. The book's publication was a kind of coming out for my union with the energy. In truth, we had written the book together. Or, perhaps more accurate to say, my experience with the energy provided its raw material, which I then translated into manuscript form. But that's not quite right to say either, because the energy was also fully infused within me during the creation of every single sentence. So, in that sense, the book truly was a joint venture. The launch of *Unconditional Bliss* was me presenting us. We both knew it, even if almost no one else did.

One person who did know was Hannah. In the fall of 2000 she was living in San Diego, which is where one of my first public workshops was scheduled. Even though we weren't seeing or speaking to each other much by that time, it still felt exactly right to be sharing the moment with her. She sat supportively in the back of the room, taking notes on my presentation, as I interacted with the twenty-odd people in attendance.

At the end of the event, Hannah offered constructive feedback. Each and every one of her suggestions hit home. They were easy to take in, and easy to incorporate. They reminded us how great a team we used to be. It was bittersweet to begin this new chapter of my life both with her and without her.

Soon after, by her choice, Hannah and I fell out of touch. Except for my offer to share a prepublication draft of this book with her, which she declined, we haven't connected in more than fifteen years.

But the energy and I, well, we were just getting started.

EPILOGUE

From the beginning, I sought to capture You in words. It's never been possible, but just giving up wasn't possible either. You changed everything—my experience of being alive, my perception of what life is, and my understanding of what life is for. How could I not bear witness to that, no matter how flawed or insufficient my efforts?

My first attempt to bear witness came in the form of journaling. I wrote fevered renderings of our early encounters as soon as possible after they occurred. I struggled to complete them before each unbelievable twist would blot out the one that came before. These entries comprise hundreds of pages. I labeled them as the "K" file. I dutifully transferred that file, over the ensuing twenty years, each time I bought a new computer. Still, at one point the file was mysteriously lost. I would have been devastated, but luckily I'd also saved a hard copy.

Rereading that hard copy led me to understand that it was time to move beyond just writing about You privately. I also needed to share. You, me, us. I needed to reveal the whole affair in spite of all the reasons not to. I needed to sacrifice my fear of exposure for the greater good of an unvarnished accounting. So, one at a time, I scanned those hundreds of pages back into digital, searchable form.

The painstaking scanning process created an unintentional but perfect ritual to mark the commencement of this book. It acted within me as a slow, deliberate crossing from the decades of knowing that someday I *might* tell our story to the new reality of actually doing it. It marked my decision to fall backward into the story in order to bring forward the next, and likely final, chapter of my life. In this final chapter, I understood, our union would become fully, phantasmagorically public.

And now, we're almost there. My final task is to sketch a brief portrait of our life together since the years covered in this book. In doing so I need to once again address our reader, and to answer what seems like the biggest remaining question:

After all that's happened, who do I now identify as "me"?

Addressing this question takes us back into the realm of paradox. Here, we recognize that all is One, but that the One manifests itself in infinite variety. Here, the Relative and the Absolute are simultaneously opposite and indivisible. Here, there is no separate self which can be located among the endless stream of thoughts, sensations, and perceptions we experience throughout our lives, yet clearly from birth to death we each exist as individual organisms that bear persistent, distinctive traits.

In my case, I believe, a splinter of the One woke up in me when the circumstances and timing were just right. Whether referred to as "Kundalini" or "the energy," it came from the Absolute side of the paradox. It is luminous with divinity, explosive with universal force. However—and this is key—it also has its own personality. It turned out to be more a god than God, even though it has direct access to spiritual power in a way that humans don't. In this godly form, though limitless, it is also replete with limitations. For example, early in our journey it could not keep demonic energy from riding in on its coattails. Plus, it has often been raw, crude, and even immature in its methods. The unique paradox of this divine interloper renders it both superb teacher and holy rogue.

In this regard, I don't resonate completely with Joan Shivarpita Harrigan's assertion, shared at the end of chapter 13, that it was a pure manifestation of Shakti I was dancing with the whole time. I don't view the movement of prana through me as directed with divine precision. Maybe Shakti oversaw the process, or intervened from time to time, but it seems to be a much more anarchic spirit, equal parts confounding and compelling, that was engaging with me in the day-to-day.

By now I've come to own that spirit, whether it originally emanated from within me or outside me, in the sense of being responsible for its actions without taking credit for its gifts. By now I've come to recognize and accept that it has altered the me I used to be in nearly every way imaginable. If it left tomorrow, as a catalyst removes itself from a chemical reaction, I'd likely find myself with as much of its own personality as the one I'd called mine before.

Here and now, in the moment of this writing, I find the sense of "me" as indistinguishable from the energy. I find myself discernible only *in relationship* to it. The more I devote myself to that relationship, the more the me of today effortlessly, paradoxically shines forth. The more I seek to assert any sense of self apart from that relationship, the more my identity becomes lifeless, dissonant, and indistinct.

Through its wildness, my relationship with the energy has made me more gentle. Through its relentless pressure, my relationship with the energy has made me more spacious. Through its bizarre and unclassifiable expression, my relationship with the energy has made me able to honor others in their own experiences "beyond the pale."

The energy has never stood in my way on this side of the pale either. As I slowly became its ambassador here in the realm of consensus reality, it always let me lead. For all its chaotic force, it didn't disrupt any of the books I've written, the hundreds of workshops I've held, or the thousands of client sessions I've facilitated. Whenever I've needed it to take a backseat to the needs of others, or to the moment at hand, it quieted without protest.

In addition, the energy never erased any of my primary traits. To those not in the know, even people with whom I interact regularly, I still seem like the same guy I've always been. While I'm definitely a little eccentric, most people assess me as more similar to them than different. As far as I can tell, from the feedback I've received, there isn't any spiritual otherness in how I come across. I tend to blend in easily at the supermarket, on the basketball court, at coffee houses and nightclubs.

Over the years, the energy has come to ask less and less of me. I no longer need hours a day to support its flow through the sinews of my body and the knots of my being. In fact, I rarely need to carve out quality time just for us. It finds me for that in sleep, or in long road trips when my singing becomes a portal to its primal yowls. When I meet others in the depth of presence that the energy taught me to recognize, the energy still shows up, too, but with respect and deference now rather than its previous wanton hunger for more, more, more.

In many ways we're like an old couple that has been together forever. Our union has become more important than either of us individually. We find the rough edges between us mostly amusing. Sappy as it is to say, we really do finish each other's sentences.

Reflecting on the energy and me, I've stumbled upon a humbling realization. Our relationship, for all its traumas and challenges, is the longest one I've ever had. I couldn't find a way to make two marriages work. My other love affairs, no matter how short or long, tumbled off one cliff or another. Only the energy and I, strikingly, have managed to remain aloft.

How did this happen? How does it keep happening? My first answer is that I don't know. And that I don't need to know. And that not knowing is our sanctified terrain. But something else comes to me, too. I think, remarkably, that all the chaos and turmoil kept thrusting us back together. Each mysterious and maddening rupture, each staggering crisis of faith, led us to reforge a stronger bond. Improbable though it seems, the "crazy" was our glue.

Some don't survive this, I know. Their crazy is anything but glue. They end up broken by Spirit's heedless force. They end up misdiagnosed, drugged, institutionalized, or driven to take their own lives. It's a miracle that what woke up in me took a form that was just enough crazy, and just the right form of crazy, to break me open but keep me sane.

Before concluding, I need to share what matters most to me about the journey I've recounted. The opening of my heart, through this whole mysterious explosion, allowed me to become intimate with life in a brand new way. It allowed me to attune to other people, and to what connects us all, which in turn engenders healing and wholeness.

Graced by what woke me up, I became able to accompany people through unimaginable pain. As this loving presence flows through me, it supports people in finally overcoming whatever wounding had previously seemed insurmountable. When my partners in presence reveal the most raw and challenging parts of their human experience, it's always as much a gift to me as it is to them.

Feeling is healing, I've been shown again and again, and when such feeling is shared within a compassionate connection, the very axis of existence seems to shift into more harmonious alignment.

As a young boy to whom people naturally gravitated for support, the seeds of sacred accompaniment were already within me. But it was the energy, and my union with it, that fertilized this potential and transformed it into an enduring vocation.

I am anything but alone in this role as a healing presence. Our fractured world is held together by countless others, dedicated, often unrecognized, who administer the art of radical attunement. But without my visitation from the energy, without question, I wouldn't have had the precious opportunity to become one of them. Nor would I have had the chance to share what underlies such attunement in my books, workshops, and beyond.

In the end, to survive the divine I had to entwine the divine. And it had to entwine me. Now, always, in every moment, we are entwining one another. Through this dance I've recognized that every one of us, you included, whether you know it or not, is divine in the same bewilderingly magnificent way. Your union with the divine is complete, yet somehow still unfolding, even as you long for it to be.